TESTIMONIALS

"Andrea has a way about her that enables you to fully confront and admit all the things that you might not have noticed all on your own. She helps you see clarity and gives you strength to make changes, big or small. She is amazing because she radiates positivity and truthfulness and makes it possible to be your own self-advocate. I feel lucky to know her and have her in my daily life. Thank you for everything Andrea!"

— Hannah Oehl

"Last year after 3 back surgeries and one being a spinal cord stimulator I could no~ ~~~ ~~~ ~f ~~~. Now that I found Andrea Gross I bike ride 4-5 times t 51 years old."

— John McKeon

"Upliftin : than once, found me when I had given-up all hope. New directions....new beginnings ~ a lifestyle coach that has been there, and can relate."

— Rima Apanavicius,
Ormond Beach, FL

9-15

When You're Ready

Andrea Gross

BALBOA.
PRESS
A DIVISION OF HAY HOUSE

Balboa Press books may be ordered through booksellers or by contacting:

Balboa Press
A Division of Hay House
1663 Liberty Drive
Bloomington, IN 47403
www.balboapress.com
1-(877) 407-4847

ISBN: 978-1-4525-4221-8 (sc)
ISBN: 978-1-4525-4222-5 (hc)
ISBN: 978-1-4525-4223-2 (e)

Library of Congress Control Number: 2011961879

Because of the dynamic nature of the Internet, any web addresses or links contained in this book may have changed since publication and may no longer be valid. The views expressed in this work are solely those of the author and do not necessarily reflect the views of the publisher, and the publisher hereby disclaims any responsibility for them.

The author of this book does not dispense medical advice or prescribe the use of any technique as a form of treatment for physical, emotional, or medical problems without the advice of a physician, either directly or indirectly. The intent of the author is only to offer information of a general nature to help you in your quest for emotional and spiritual well-being. In the event you use any of the information in this book for yourself, which is your constitutional right, the author and the publisher assume no responsibility for your actions.

Any people depicted in stock imagery provided by Thinkstock are models, and such images are being used for illustrative purposes only.
Certain stock imagery © Thinkstock.

Printed in the United States of America

Balboa Press rev. date: 2/7/2012

A Special Dedication

Someone very close to me once said during my darkest hour, *"Don't give in."* Those three words have carried me through to today. I knew I was no longer fighting for myself, nor was I alone.

Thank you!

From the movie *Waiting to Exhale*:

"Count on Me"

"There's a place inside all of us where our faith in love begins.
You must reach to find the truth in love—the answer's there within.
I know that life can make you feel it's much harder than it really is,
But you'll get through it, just don't give in."

Always remember to be strong and to love yourself first and foremost. It isn't selfish; it is vital for a happy and healthy life. No matter what anyone else tells you, you are enough, you are good enough, and you have everything you need. Just believe it.

Dedications

This book is dedicated to many people, but most of all to my kids, Corey, Jordan, and Drew, whose love and support has carried me through some extremely rough days. I know in my heart that although they have suffered, they have helped me to break the cycle for their children and for future generations to come. I love them with all of my heart and am so proud of them. Because of them, I am a better person today.

I dedicate this book to my dog Jack as well. Although he is no longer with us, he sat by my side watching me write every night. He rubbed his head on my leg when I cried and got excited when I laughed. He was there through every high and every low, unconditionally. He will always be with me.

I also dedicate this to my two grandmothers, whose suffering I never understood until I got divorced and began to grow. Although their lives were difficult, I know there were many days I gave them joy. I think I knew all along.

I also dedicate this to my parents, who love me unconditionally. As a family, we have been through a lot, not only presently but back then as well. I love them both very much, and I wish them both love, peace, and happiness.

I dedicate this to my sister as well. Although we missed so much growing up, I treasure her love and friendship. All in all, she was and is my "go-to" person.

I also dedicate this to my BFFs (you know who you are) and to Robyn, my best friend from high-school. Although Robyn has passed away, I know she is still with me and cheering me on. Each of these women has been with me every step of the way. They are each unique in what they have contributed, but they all have given me unconditional love and support. We have spent many hours laughing and crying, and without them I do not know where I would be. They have taught me how to have and be a true-blue friend.

I also dedicate this book to the men you will be reading about. Each one of them will always be a soul mate to me, because each in his own way has helped me get to where I am today. I will always be grateful that God brought them into my life. I am even more grateful that, painfully, I have figured out why and have moved on. I pray that someday they will learn everything I have learned and have healthy, loving relationships of their own. Some of them are now friends, some are still question marks, and some I no longer speak to.

Speaking of men, I also want to thank my brother-in-law, who has been a strong shoulder for me to lean on. He is always there whenever I need him and always makes my kids and I laugh. You know the clown at family dinners who makes it all fun? That's him. He makes me feel like everything is going to be okay!

Now for my Thank-Yous.

First of all, I must thank my life coach from way back, Cameron. He not only helped me figure it all out, but he is also the reason I became a lifestyle coach.

Next, I thank Aimee Raupp, my acupuncturist, whose bimonthly facial acupuncture has completely changed my skin and set the clock back! After a treatment with Aimee, I feel radiant from the inside out. Thanks, Aimee, for all the client referrals as well!

Thank you to my photographer, Laura Bruen, who I began working with over three years ago. She saw something in me through her lens before I even did! I recommend to everyone reading this to get your makeup and hair professionally done and have your very own photo shoot. Once someone else sees your beauty, you begin to see it yourself.

I have to thank my publicist, Elaine. She is always there with encouragement and inspires me to keep going! She's also a great friend.

I also want to thank Sharon for her endless support and devotion to my children. It is not easy to maintain relationships with your in laws when you get divorced, although we went through a rough patch, I thank her for remembering who I am.

I owe another thank-you to my clients and fans. Thank you for trusting me and believing in what I say. I hope that through my story, I can continue to guide you so that you can live authentic lives and always feel beautiful and strong. For my fans who post their comments and likes daily, you guys inspire me every morning to sign on to Facebook and say what's on my mind! Always know that I have been in your shoes and have my good days and bad days as well. Just knowing my posts can help you get through your days is priceless to me.

I thank God for white roses, vanilla candles, and Dark Reese cups! I also thank him for giving me the strength to get through it all—although sometimes I was angry that he was giving me too much to handle at once!

Lastly, this book is dedicated to the love of my life, my true soul mate. You are the one I learned to "want" instead of "need." This is for you, the one I grew up for—the one I changed my life for. I know you have been through the same things that I have, and we "get" each other. We can grow old together but stay young at heart; we can laugh together, adore each other, and cherish every day of our new lives. I can't wait to wake up next to you every day!

CONTENTS

INTRODUCTION

"When you're ready" can mean anything you need it to mean. Whatever it means to you today could change by the time you finish reading this book. Things keep changing for me every day. There are no guarantees; the only constant is my commitment to myself.

My story can help you be ready for anything you dream about. Maybe you're ready to lose weight and finally have your dream body, regardless of your age. After all, every one of us has a sexy inner diva; we just have layers of self-doubt covering her up! Maybe you're ready to divorce and move on with your life. Or maybe you're ready to improve your marriage.

I think it's a matter of finding yourself first. That way, what you are unhappy about becomes clearer. First work on yourself, and the decisions will come naturally—when you're ready.

People have been asking me over the last year what my book is about. For some reason, I have a hard time coming up with a standard answer. It is about so many different things: conquering fear, being a mom, my "hopelessly romantic" dreams, overcoming major setbacks, and love.

But it is mostly about breaking the cycle. It's about creating a new world for my children and saying things my grandmothers and the generations before them were too afraid to say.

This book is about helping people with my own story. It is about showing you that we are all human, flawed, damaged, or whatever else you want to call it. It is a story about hope, love, and passion. To me, these are the three most important things there are in life. Without them, we hardly exist. At age forty-seven, I decided to choose a different path for myself, which at times was very agonizing. The end result was a success. If I hadn't made that choice, you would not be reading my story. If this book inspires you to live your life with passion, then I have succeeded. I wish you a happy, authentic life!

This book is happy, sad, funny, and honest. I have learned through many hardships that the only way to truly be happy is to be yourself. I have learned that your true friends not only know that but embrace it, no matter what they think. They are there to laugh and cry with you. I have learned that true friends will feel your pain, but at the same time they will remind you that everything will work out.

I now know not to take things too seriously. Even though other people's issues and insecurities might hurt us, we learn from them. We do not have to be victims of them. I've learned that the most important thing in life is to love ourselves because it is the only way we can ever love someone else. I also know that even if we have the worst possible day, it can all change in a split second if we are open to change.

I am a true believer in manifestation. I believe that you can create the life and love you want in your mind. If you believe with all of your heart that your dreams will come true, then they will. I know that some of my dreams didn't exactly work out the way I thought they would because they weren't supposed to. I know that making my wish board and reading it every night before bed helped to make it my reality.

Enjoy my story, but, most importantly, enjoy your own.

When I started writing this book, urged by my friends and my sister who spent endless, and I mean *endless*, hours talking, crying, and laughing with me, the only thing I was sure of was that I had to focus on my three kids and get them to a stable, healthy place. I had to learn to really love and reinvent myself, but those were just words, I *really* had no idea how. So like many of you, I went to Barnes and Noble every week and read every book I could find about self-love and moving on. I wanted to know how to do it. *Where do I start? Can't someone explain it so I can understand it?* Most of the books were too spiritual, too technical, or too corny. Some I loved and some I felt I could have written better. I decided to start writing my story so that one day someone would come to Barnes and Noble like I did, wanting to know what it was really like to start over. I wanted to tell people what it felt like to connect and smile again. I wanted people to know how I took care of myself dispite indigestion, anxiety, and a benign tumor. I wanted people to know what worked for me and why I feel better, prettier, and younger at fifty than I ever have. I decided the person who was going to write the book was me.

Thirty years ago I had *big* dreams of being a film editor. Like my uncle in the film business, I always loved movies and the Hollywood/celebrity world always intrigued me. I can tell you about any celeb even before *People* comes out! Anyway, I went to Syracuse University and signed up to minor in Newhouse (as in SI—*the* most prestigious film school). My first class was a film editing class but being nineteen and immature, concerned more about my social life and partying, I dropped out of my first film class and walked out on my dream of being in the movie industry. I did however major in clothing/retailing and ended up opening my own children's clothing boutique, which was very successful and it allowed my husband to start his own business.

Today after twenty years of marriage, a divorce, three kids, and three businesses, my old dream is alive again. My dream is that this book, or maybe the next one, becomes a movie one day. I do not know what my future holds, but I do know that timing is everything and that sometimes dreams do come back, and so do people. When I started this book I had some different friends, a different home, and a different life. I am not completely sure where I am going, but I do know I am on the right road . . . because I am happy.

So, just remember timing is everything in life and love. The universe already knows your game plan. There will be some great days and some very painful ones, but I believe we all get there eventually; it doesn't really matter when or how. This book will help you prepare for whatever your dreams are.

As far as love goes, I know we all have many soul mates in life and sometimes the ones we thought were the right ones were merely lessons we needed to learn. I just wish they didn't have to be so painful.

So prepare to laugh and cry! Most importantly, I hope reading my story is the beginning of your new journey, whatever it may be. My intention in writing this is to make you realize that anything and everything is possible. You just have to believe in your dreams and love yourself. It sounds simple, but it is not easy for most of us. I hope my book simplifies the process for you.

Before you begin, you need to know I am a true believer in manifestation. For those of you who don't understand what that is, it's believing in something so strongly that you even live as if it has already happened and this is what, in turn, brings it to you. I manifested writing this book, living in a new house, a new bedroom, one of my books becoming a movie, and the guy on my Tiffany-framed wish board hanging in my room.

Enjoy!

BACKGROUND

I think that it's important for everyone reading this to know a little bit about my background and why I made the choices that I did. Without going into too much detail, growing up in my house was a bit challenging for me. I was the oldest of three and my brother and sister were only a year apart and were very close. I was the big "bossy" sister. I was always very social and always had a boyfriend. On the outside, we had the perfect family: we had a second home in Colorado, a pool and a tennis court, and got whatever we wanted, but there was something painfully missing. I struggled with the lack of attention, connection, and affection in my home and began to express myself through writing and poetry. I expressed myself this way because I had no other outlet, besides my friends. I did see a therapist when I was in high school because my parents really had no idea why I acted out so much. At the time, nobody understood why I was angry—after all, I had the "perfect life." However, it wasn't until I got divorced that I started to understand a lot more about my childhood.

Don't get me wrong: my parents loved me the best that they could, but there was a lack of connection in my house. My parents had the typical marriage. Mom was home, Dad worked hard and traveled a lot for business, and they spent their Saturday nights going out with other couples. I noticed they never really showed much affection, nor did they have good communication skills, but, like so many married people of their generation, they "dealt with it." I knew that someday my marriage was going to be different and I would communicate not only with my spouse but with my children in a better way. I knew I was going to stay home and raise my kids as opposed to taking the career and live-in nanny route, and with a husband who was going to be my best friend. I would only marry someone one day who I had a connection with and who I could talk to. We all dream about the perfect marriage and spouse, but when we come from a dysfunctional home we really have no idea what it feels like. We just think we do.

Fast-forward to college, this is where I met my ex-husband. He and his roommate and I and mine were best friends. We spent hours every day laughing and having fun. I was closer to all of them than I have ever been to anyone. To make a long story short, my boyfriend at the time was a friend of theirs and we all spent a lot of time together. By senior year, we realized we were not only great friends but we were attracted to each other, there was great chemistry. We had a very tumultuous relationship. We were constantly on and off. When we graduated, he moved to NYC and wanted to live the single life. I wanted to get engaged. I was busy starting my own business and only wanted to get married and start my family with him. It wasn't until I began dating other people that he turned around. We went through years of make-ups and break-ups, and I think "getting married" became more of an issue than whether or not we belonged together. I spent hours crying but still wanted him. We never really had good communication.

Once we became engaged, everything fit into place. We got married, started having children, and, after many happy years, although I loved him dearly, I think we slowly began to grow apart and I began to lose myself. I became afraid to be myself and speak my mind and he was afraid to let me change. He wanted everything to stay the same so desperately and I started to feel like I was going to die if things did not change. We were both struggling with our own unhappy childhoods and to top it off, we had horrible communication skills. I pushed and pushed for therapy but he wanted no part of it. As you know, my quest to find the answers led me to a life coach, and eventually, after my own life-changing experience with a coach, a certification, and a lot of self-work . . . Andrea Gross, Lifestyle Coach, was born, and is thriving today.

It's important to mention that I have no regrets even though the "being married forever" dream of mine was shattered. I never in a zillion years thought I would ever be divorced, but life happens and people do grow and change. Sometimes when we are angry and going through the divorce process we have doubts and fears and think, *How could we possibly end this, even if it's not good?* But something inside called your "soul" takes over and guides you. It guides you, along with your heart, through every day and every week until you get to a place where you feel safe and you are able to breathe on your own.

My idea of the right husband or soul mate has changed so much because I have changed. Even from the first day I sat down to write this book until today (two years later) it has drastically changed. Just throughout the last six months I have added things to my soul-mate wish list, such as "emotionally stable" (one I had never even understood) and "has my back." Since being on my own, I have met some really great people. I have become more secure and confident and am now a much better communicator. Yes, I have days I cry or lose my cool with my kids, but I am only human.

I still believe that being best friends and having great physical attraction is vital in any relationship, but I also now know there has to be a lot more to it. There has to be a level of respect for the other person and you have to be secure enough with yourself to let the other person shine and do his or her own thing (and only someone who is shining himself would understand that). Controlling someone is a sign of insecurity and will only break up a relationship eventually. I also know that, regardless of who works, who brings home the most money, etc., everything is equal. I am a modern mom and modern woman so the June Cleaver thing doesn't work for me. I enjoy myself and being alone (sometimes) and revel in preparing for my next soul mate. I do anticipate with love and know great love is on the way. I am sure whoever it is will have gone through this kind of transformation because it is the only way he will understand what I have been through, and we will love and treasure each other that much more for it. Being alone is a stepping stone for any successful relationship and I have definitely had my fair share!

I now know that I had to be alone. I had to give myself the love that had been missing since childhood. I had to be alone to learn to love and respect myself so I would know what it felt like. I had to get my confidence back, which I did. I had to go through feeling like a lonely, damaged, ex-wife to feeling like a single, pretty, woman who has so much to offer and so much love to give (after giving it to herself). I had to feel beautiful, sexy, and alive again, even though the clock was ticking. I had to get my body ready to have "new" sex. I had to figure out how to be happy and stay young looking, especially because I like youthful men. I had to learn how to be a single parent, be my own accountant, get my own insurance . . . I did it all and much, much more.

MY LIFE COACH AND
COMING FULL CIRCLE

My decision to become a lifestyle coach came from my experiences and from going through the coaching process. I was in such a confused state and had seen various therapists, but it wasn't until I Googled "life coach" one day that things began to change. I no longer wanted to talk about the past; I wanted help with how to move forward. I knew I was scared to death but could not understand why. I Googled the number one coaching company (I always go right to the top!) and read its president's bio. Cameron was mainly a business coach, but there were other coaches within his company (with specialties in weight loss, relationships, divorces, etc.). After speaking to him for a while, he suggested I try one of the women coaches but I said, "No, I only want to work with you." He told me he would have to see if he could fit me into his schedule. Mind you, this guy coaches corporations, and here I was a scared housewife from New Jersey begging for his help. I was relentless. I only wanted to work with him. He was intelligent and great to talk to. We spoke on the phone once a week; I lived on the East Coast and he on the West Coast. I began to realize how great it was to speak to a man who really "got it" and understood men. I was able to express my true feelings and fears and he was the first person who was able to inspire me to dig deep down and do what I wanted to do, even though neither one of us knew what that was. With coaching, you help people to figure out on their own what they want. I decided while working with him that I would become certified and be a coach so I could help others like he had helped me. He even told me once that I would be a great coach. Coaching had changed my life and my goal was to help others change theirs.

We all know that I did get to a great place, eventually. The same way that everything in life comes full circle, so did my coach and I. This past summer, almost three years since I filed for divorce, he emailed that he was coming to New York and wanted to meet. We ended up meeting. He was now in the very place that I was in when I was working with him: he was getting a divorce. Now I was the one with the words of encouragement for him. As we spoke, I realized that I was ready to take my coaching to another level. Here I was giving *my* words of wisdom to my coach.

A few weeks ago, Cameron forwarded me an email from a woman in New Jersey who was looking for a coach. He recommended me. I guess he realized when we met that I was ready. After all, he was one of the top coaches in the country. It was quite an honor. After speaking to the woman and sending her to my website to read my story, she asked if I would come and speak to a group of women that she would be putting together once a month. I told her I would be happy to. Not only has my life come full circle, but my dream of becoming a lifestyle coach has turned into a career as well. I am finally doing what I love to do. I have found my passion and it is working for me.

Five years ago I was miserable and I had no idea what to do with myself. I was passionless and now I have a career I love that I started all on my own. I'll never forget listening to Oprah say, "If you do something you are passionate about, you will always make money." Here I am: I never gave up even when I had no idea how I would ever get clients. I spent money on a publicist and I had no income. I believed in myself and there was no way I was giving up. Yes, to make things easier I could have gotten a part-time job, but I hung in there and worked and worked and here I am with my own business. My determination pursued throughout the stress of my divorce, through recuperating from my benign tumor, my parents' divorce, getting two teenagers and a tween through a divorce, the loss of my dog . . . I could go on and on but the point is I made it. Not only did I make it, but I am sharing my story to give all of you hope and faith with whatever you are going through.

MR. X

My definition of Mr. X: He can be anyone who has ever touched you in a way that changed your life or woke you up. It can be someone who once gave you a compliment, it can be a friend, a lover, a stranger, or even someone in your imagination who you dream about. I've had many Mr. X's in my life. Some were real and some I haven't even met yet.

Sometimes a real Mr. X will pop into your life at just the right time to give you a sign (soul mate). Although they may have a huge affect on your life, it can be painful when they all of a sudden disappear. Do not be upset about it and take from it the lesson it was meant to teach you. Be open to Mr. X's in your life, because they will ultimately lead you to the right soul mate. When it's the real Mr. X, you will just know it because it will be mutual, easy, and your mind, body, and soul will just feel that it is right. Do not ever settle. All three have to be there for a happy relationship. Body (physical chemistry), mind (personality), and soul (how they make you feel)—nothing more and nothing less! Most importantly, you will be with your true soul mate only when you can be your true self. It won't happen the right way until you are.

If you start manifesting, as I will discuss later, you will get used to the feeling of your *real* Mr. X before he even arrives. That way, when he does, you will be comfortable and he will seem familiar to you. The only way to be happy with another person is if you are really being your authentic self and vice versa. This way you inspire each other to grow because insecurities aren't in the way.

Another definition before you begin is *recovery*—a vital stage to get to and be in before you move on. In recovery, you forgive and understand why. The amount of time spent in recovery varies for everyone; I was in it for a very long time, the wounds were deep.

Whether you are single, divorced, or married, I hope my book inspires you to love yourself because I know what that can do to your love life! I wish everyone who reads this love and happiness.

XOXO
Andrea

THE DECISION

The summer was beginning; it was Memorial Day Weekend, my anniversary, and my husbands birthday. All three kids were in LA with their aunt. I wasn't happy at this point but wasn't 100 percent sure it was because of my marriage . . . yet. I was determined to try to turn things around, even though I can't really tell you why. The more I was told, "It's your fault and you are just a miserable, ungrateful person," the more I began to realize why I was so unhappy. Hello?

Yes, I was unhappy because my passion and liveliness had been suppressed for so long. I wasn't myself anymore. I was afraid to speak up and be my own person. I knew deep down that I could not do this forever. Things had to change.

The romance and passion had disappeared and my husband and I began going through the motions. I realized a lot that weekend. I realized I needed more. I needed depth. I needed to share myself with someone who felt like I did. I wanted to be with someone who felt as alive as I did and who let me be all I could be. I needed someone who had a shining heart light so we could shine together.

I was too afraid to do anything, but this unhappiness began to build and build. I tried going through the motions to keep the peace for my kids, but after a while I realized, *What am I really doing for my kids? If I am not happy and I am with someone who is not willing to do anything to understand or change this, how will my kids ever understand relationships and love?* This is where so many of us get stuck—is it better for kids to grow up in an unloving environment just to have their parents under one roof? The answers to me began to get clearer and clearer. How can I be my authentic self and be the best mom I can be while living a lie? It was torture being so torn every day. I do not want to go into details out of respect for my children and my ex, but we all know what I finally decided.

I now know that I will never live with those feelings and fear again. I live with a lot of pain still knowing my ex wasn't willing to get the help that he needed for his pain and that letting me walk out was easier for him. However, I know now it all worked out for the best, for me.

Anyway, it is three years later and I have been divorced for a year and a half and it took until now to understand why I have not been ready for a relationship. I had a revelation today that helped me understand why. A therapist helping me with my kids said, "Andrea, you could have a boyfriend any minute of any day. You have been through so much. Why is it that you think you don't think you're ready?" I sat for a few minutes and began to cry. They were happy tears just as much as they were sad tears. I had just in that moment figured out why I would still rather be home working on this book or watching a movie on my cozy, romantic bed by myself on Saturday night. The therapist looked me in the eye and said, "You've been through so much, you are still in recovery." I cried, knowing a real professional had acknowledged what it was. I now had the answer not only for myself but for anyone else who had asked why I wasn't ready. I admitted to myself that day that parts of my marriage took their toll on me and I was scared of repeating it. It doesn't matter what anyone thinks because I know the truth about my life. I know the truth and I know I have given myself a new chance. I know I need to forgive myself for what I have been through. I had to forgive myself for not respecting myself enough. Now, I know I have come a long way and know exactly what I want.

I am writing this book not to condemn my ex or anyone else. Most of us have our darkness. My self-work has now become about emotionally detaching from anything that is not good for me. I walked to my car after that therapy session doing an exercise in my mind. I cut all ties to anyone and everyone who had not treated me well. I understand I knew nothing differently with men and accepted more than I ever will again. I know, as I get stronger and stronger, I will get closer and closer to real love. First I will have to dig deep and honor my dignity and self-esteem by emotionally detaching. I need to do this for my children and myself. I cannot be fighting with my ex anymore. For anyone reading this who is divorced and still fighting with their ex, please get the help you need, swallow your pride, and do it for your kids. Believe me, there have been times he triggered me so badly I could be in jail right now just for thinking about what I wanted to do. You have to stop thinking things will change and change the way you react. If things were bad when you were married, they will not be better when you are divorced. I do pray that someday we will be able to be friends and I send love and include him in my prayers, but as of today, I am determined to detach emotionally and permanently.

This is a huge thing for me to finally be ready to let go and see what the other side of love can look like. I know I have been dreaming about it for years. Now when I manifest I have a clear vessel to work with. Until now it was clogged with old energy. As I get freer from the emotional pull, I will get closer to my own reality. I think until now I was afraid to admit I was in recovery. I think it is similar to a drug addict or an alcoholic. I no longer have to hide. I can face what really happened and move on. I know it is okay to have the pain I live with and to cry because I am releasing it. Releasing helps make it go away. I tell my kids all the time that crying is good because it's better to get it out. I hope I am saving them from pain later on and I know that the stronger I get, the better it will be for them.

It's important for me to mention that most of my married years were good ones and my children were born during those happy times. Unfortunately, sometimes people change and grow apart.

I am really starting to come alive; I feel better than ever. Coming out of the dark is invigorating. Leaving an unhappy marriage is one of the most challenging things a woman can face, especially when the other person is so angry he can't even let himself understand his problems. However, after two years I have learned not to take it personally and not to get emotional about it. Believe it or not, I have been divorced eight months already and still get the nasty emails and text messages. Technology is good and bad for divorced people—good because you do not have to talk to each other, but bad because it's a way to maintain contact.

BACK TO MR. X

This story is not being written to scare you, it's being written to show you there is hope. By writing this, I kept the faith, hope, and intention alive. I need to explain how possible it is for someone who hardly knows you to be able to help you change your life in such an intense way that you begin to grow and live the life you were meant to live. You get to a point where you don't mind being single; you kind of start liking it. God, so many friends and people I know are still living a surreal life. I feel so lucky that I am not. Instead of looking at the older couples in restaurants or out taking a walk and being resentful, I am hopeful. I have changed so much. I look at them and am happy for them and it makes me look forward to my next love, which will be such a different love because I am so different. I am forty-eight and am not full grown so I want my next relationship to be one where we can both grow separately but adore the time together.

Anyway, getting back to that special someone who literally changed my life, I think a lot of people have different soul mates in their lives. Today I am a better person, mother, sister, everything. I am a better person because I love myself, and because of that I can love others more fully and greater than I ever did before. Because of this self-love, people look at me differently. Some are envious and jealous, but my true-blue friends are happy for me and tell me how proud they are of me all the time, and that is what has gotten me through the most challenging times. The best part is my new relationship with my kids. We are closer than ever because I can be myself with them. I don't have anyone arguing with me in front of them. It's really cool, especially since my kids are getting older.

Back to soul mate. I started to get in touch with my senses again, the senses that had been numbed by a destructive relationship that I ignored for so many years. Through their own pain, they were able to help me transform. A lot of the advice I never understood until a few years later when I was in the same boat they had once been in, when I had to cry buckets of tears on my own. Sometimes I would reread all the text messages from one in particular. I knew somehow he was guiding me along. His sense of humor sometimes made me laugh so deeply that I would practically pee in my pants. God, it made me realize that I had stopped laughing. I really needed to laugh and be funny without anyone telling me "I wasn't".

What is so confusing and hard about the Mr. X thing is not knowing whether it was real or not. I had not been in the single scene since after college and had no idea what a "player" was. To me, if someone was texting and calling and saying nice things, they were sincere. But, I knew I did not leave my marriage for anyone other than myself.

SATURDAY NIGHT WITH LEBRON

I met my friend for brunch today in the city. She asked me about last night (Saturday) and I told her about my night and she was crying and laughing and said, "You have to put this in your book!" So here it goes . . .

It's just a typical Saturday night for me. I had no plans but my daughter had a bat mitzvah in Times Square and I didn't want to take her, come home, and go back, so I planned on dropping her off, taking a cab to Lincoln Square to treat myself to two hours of Vince Vaughn *(Couples Retreat),* getting something to eat, and picking her up at eleven to go home. Good plan, right? Simple.

Not really! Have you ever been to Times Square on a beautiful Saturday night? It wasn't the theater traffic that was so bad; it was the mobs and mobs of people walking around! There were so many people I couldn't even drive. My daughter was a half hour late so I pulled into a parking lot thinking I would drop her off and try to get a cab. My movie was starting at eight, it was seven, and I needed to get there and eat something. I was starving! There were no cabs in sight. I had to get uptown otherwise I would have to spend the next four hours in the M&M store! All of a sudden one of those guys on a bike pulls up. I ask him if he's in good enough shape to ride thirty blocks in twenty minutes. He says, "No problem!" Of course it wasn't a problem: he charged me thirty-five dollars!

Anyway, here I am Saturday night, sitting in the back of this thing, hundreds of people are watching me, and he puts on his music! He's blasting the song from *Arthur* and people are waving at me like I am some celebrity. I am dying, humiliated beyond belief, but here's the great part: I am laughing, not crying, because everyone is watching me on Saturday night ride alone through the streets of NYC. I have really gotten to a good place. I'm okay, thank God. I get to the movie theater just in time. I will buy a ticket, pee, get candy (no time for healthy food), and get my seat. Guess what? Sold out! I try my credit card three times. I even buy a ticket for the later show and try to switch it. No shot. My only options are to go to a bar, that's not happening! Or see *More Than a Game,* the Lebron James movie. So I end up seeing Lebron.

What a great film! I loved it. I was texting my boys throughout the whole movie. It was such a great experience. I never would have seen it if everything had worked out. It just goes to show, girls, sometimes we have to take another road that leads us to a place we never would have gone. If I had been depressed and feeling insecure, I would have gone home and come back to pick up my daughter, but I made the best of it and it turned out okay. I think of it as a sign that everything is going to be okay.

Tomorrow I am signing the papers to sell my house, making a deal on the townhouse, and my website is ready and amazing. When I saw the intro to my website, I cried I was so proud of myself for how hard I have been working on it. This weekend is the seminar in NYC at the Soho House where I learn how to take my business forward. I can't believe everything I wanted is really falling into place. "If you build it, he will come!" (My friend cracks up from my movie quotes.) how true! I am setting the stage so everything is right. It's coming, I know it is. I will go there when I am ready and I will not be scared. I know what I want; I waited; I gave everyone the time and space they needed, especially my kids. It's going to be amazing, I can't wait to be in love and love someone again.

MR. X THE MUSE

Mr. X is my muse, he is the one getting me through every day. It is because I have hope and faith that I am doing so well. There is nothing I need to know right now. My only wish at this point is to thank him. I am so happy right now, sitting on my bed on Friday night writing my book. I need my dreams to stay dreams right now. Why give that up? Whitney Houston has a song on her new CD, the one she recorded after not singing for seven years because of the pain of her failed "abusive marriage." I blast it in my car every day. "I love you in a place where there's no space or time. I love you for my life, you are a friend of mine." You see, you can love someone from a distance, you can respect their space without being selfish about wanting them. You can learn to be patient and trust that God (my belief) and the universe are working tirelessly to make things work for you, rather than being consumed with who the right Mr. X really is. I am a different person than I was six months ago, and I am continuing to grow so who knows who will be right for me . . . one day?

I have to add this paragraph for anyone who might be fantasizing or having an emotional or even a sexual affair. Fact: 99 percent of the time they will not be the one you end up with! Affairs are affairs because they aren't reality. They are an escape from your "real" life. Sometimes even an emotional affair can show you what is missing in your marriage or relationship. You have the choice to either try to fix it or move on and eventually start all over. There are so many times I hear people saying, "They got divorced because he or she was having an affair—*not true.* Affairs are symptoms, not reasons. Affairs can temporarily replace what is missing, but at the end of the day it takes an extreme amount of courage to face reality and take the chance of being alone in hopes of finding true love. However, whether you do or you don't (you *will*) find love again, at least you will find yourself.

LAURA DAY QUOTE

Okay, so you know when you get a sign? As you become more grounded and spiritual you will get better and better at noticing them, it's really cool when it happens. For those of you who have no idea what I am talking about, it's like when you are thinking about someone and all of a sudden "your song" comes on the radio, or they drive by you, or they call you. It's kind of like mental telepathy. (It's a Laura Day thing.)

Anyway, last summer during one of my searches for answers at Barnes and Noble on Columbus (Upper West Side) I came across this workbook called *The Circle.* Now I already swore to myself I would not read anymore self-help books, but this was different. In this one, you write down your dreams in a circle—wow, how cool. I can actualy put it on paper! What you do is live your life within the circle, you can even live as if everything in the circle has already happened! Which I think I do anyway, even though I am alone now. I have this feeling all the time that I am in love—he's just not here yet! Are you laughing? I'm totally serious. When you let yourself feel love, whether there is someone in your life or not, it shows and people start to notice you more and want to know what drug you're on! Sometimes lately I am singing in my car and I catch someone looking at me like, *You go, girl!* Anyway I read in the workbook that the author, Laura Day, has these one-hour sessions at Barnes and Noble in Tribeca (how cool) that she calls the "circle group." Unfortunately, I forget about it and never go. Why am I telling you this? To get back to the point of "signs."

About six months later I was lying on my bed one night reading *Elle* magazine and there was an article about the four top women coaches and one of them was Laura Day! I quickly read it and it was all about how Demi Moore and Jen Aniston and Brad Pitt and all these famous people swear by Laura's work! Wow. I ran and dug up the workbook and started reading the dream I had written and I realized it was still the same dream; nothing had changed. Later I went on Laura's website, ordered her next book, looked up when the next meeting in Tribeca was, and signed up. If it's good enough for Demi—I'm in!

Here is a Laura quote, "I can sit with the truth and have the patience to act when I am ready for the very best outcome." I think, *Wow I have been agonizing over what I think I should do for so long and she just summed it up and made it positive.* I realized maybe I hadn't been ready for the right outcome, and that's okay. It wasn't that I was so scared I would be rejected, but maybe I was scared I was not ready. This could really work in my favor. I needed to take things slow. I was starting my business, writing this book, and moving in six weeks. So much for one little girl—who had to also take care of three kids going through such big changes in their lives! But the quote was a sign that everything was going to work out for me.

Sometimes when we are looking so hard for answers, we can't find them. It's when we stop trying so hard that God will give us a sign, and from that sign we can take it upon ourselves to figure out what it means. Our lives will develop as we interpret them. What we perceive to happen will. That's why we need to spend all this time getting it right in our minds, so we can live it in the real world. Maybe "when you're ready" means when you're ready for the very best outcome!

ATTACK OF THE MARRIED MEN

I decide that I will go out during the week for dinner with a friend—innocent enough.

It's Thursday night and I'm tired and could easily get into bed and watch *Grey's Anatomy* and my favorite show—*Private Practice*. But I'll go out and DVR them to watch Saturday night. I get dressed and feel pretty good. I'm wearing a new shirt that shows major cleavage (I'm not sure if it's too much or not) but I feel sexy so what the hell? My friend and I (she's married—married friends love to go out with me! Thank God because I have no interest in hanging out with complaining divorcees!) go to the Meatpacking District.

I love Pastis but not for the scene. I happen to love mussels and fries. They go great with my once a week Grey Goose. Anyway, we find stools at the bar, perfect because I refuse to stand at a bar (desperado). As soon as I start to sit down, my butt hasn't even hit the stool, I get *attacked by a married man!* He happened to be cute, young but not too young, smelled like a joint, and was restless. If I wanted to, I could have had this guy across the street at the Gansevoort Hotel in two seconds, but instead it was a total turnoff. He tried everything to purue me. He even

19

went so far as to show me pictures of his little yappy Maltese, which his wife (who is probably home watching *Grey's*) probably carries around in her Louis bag. I laughed and told him, "I have a Lab at home that weighs one hundred pounds who could eat that thing for breakfast." Anyway, I know it can be flattering, but like I always say, no married, getting-divorced, separated, or living-in-the-basement guys. It's my rule. I have handled myself with a lot of integrity and it will remain that way. I don't need the attention that badly. When you're in a good place, you don't compromise your standards, or settle. You can just have fun with yourself.

After drinks my friend and I go to Spice Market for dinner. It's a huge place with many tables. I am hungry and want to eat. There are a lot of couples having dinner and I get this pang: what if I see Mr. X on a date? I used to think I would just die or act like Diane Keaton in *Something's Gotta Give,* but I have it pretty together right now so I think I would just be able to say, "Hi." Right now, "being still" feels better to me than anything else, so that is where I need to stay.

There is a couple sitting right next to us that literally hasn't said one word to each other the whole night. God, I am so glad to not be sitting there. How do people live like that? How can you be in a fun restaurant and not even talk to each other? I want to say to this young couple, "Work on it now, guys. Work on it or let each other go." I had a great idea while watching them. I thought the next time I see a really great couple I am going to interview them for my book. You know, one of those great-looking, laughing, "in love" couples. The kind of couple you notice because it is so rare, they stand out like sore thumbs. It's so sad, isn't it? I can't wait to be one of those couples. I would never not be one of those couples, and that is the secret: be happy enough to want to share yourself, love yourself so much that you just want to love someone else.

GALILEO

I offer thanks to those before me . . . that's all I gotta say
Cause maybe you squandered big bucks in your lifetime . . .
now I have to pay
But then again it feels like some sort of inspiration . . .
to let the next life off the hook
"She'll say . . ." Look what I had to overcome in my last life"
I think I'll write a book . . . Galileo by the Indigo Girls

I was out on my five-mile run, listening to my daughter's iPod when this song came on—it brought tears to my eyes. Sometimes when other people say things that you are feeling, you realize you are not alone, nor are you the last person who ever had these thoughts and feelings. My children could never possibly understand right now that I have broken a painful cycle. I have no idea how painful it was for some of my relatives, nor do I know how far back it really goes. Was my great grandmother happy and with the love of her life or did she just survive and get through? There had to have been someone in my past who was a hopeless, no, forget that word, let's say hope*ful* romantic. I had to have gotten this "love" thing from somewhere other than movies. I know deep inside my soul there is deep love for my soul mate, and that I am going to help change the world with this love—if he would only get here! I bet he is having the same thoughts and revelations and he just isn't quite ready, but definitely on the right path (to my front door)! I bet he's sitting at his desk in his office dreaming about "me." He might not know me yet, but he feels me and wants to meet a girl like me very badly.

After all of this time alone, when I finally meet someone I am connected to *and* attracted to—watch out, Brangelina. You think you guys were screaming the first time! Sorry, Jen, but I can just imagine what it was like when they were finally able to "do it." There must have been some serious noise—I even remember reading in one of those celeb magazines that they were at a hotel and the staff was saying it was so noisy!

Anyway, I got way off track there! Let's get back to great grandma! What about her? As painful as this journey has been in the last few years, it is *sooo* inspirational (like the song says) to be changing history. I am changing history for my family tree. One day, when my great great grandchildren are making a family tree for school, they will write mine and my new soul mate's name on it—how great! Also on the tree will be my children with their soul mates, etc. They won't be just names. They will be actual people who are in love and showing affection every day and communicating in a positive respectful way. They will be fun and happy people, and I had something to do with it. I never get out of bed anymore without a purpose for being here.

Pre- and during my divorce, I used to have days and moments when I didn't really know why I was here. What was I supposed to be doing every day? I felt like such a loser sometimes because I had no answers. I was even believing that I was this "miserable" human being. (We won't get any further into that.) But writing this book has shown me "my purpose." I am writing this for my ancestors and my children and whoever comes after me. I am writing this for everyone who reads it. I am writing this so you can realize love is the answer to everything.

THE CANCER SCARE, SUMMER OF 2009

My kids and I were beginning to settle into "divorced life," and it was time to go for my annual GYN visit, assuming everything would be fine, as usual. My doctor, who I love, isn't taking my insurance anymore but one of the partners does, it's a woman and now that I am older I am ready for a female doctor. The doctor was giving me my regular exam and explaining to me all of the necessary precautions to take, now that I am single, and she starts feeling around on my left side *a lot!* At first I am not paying attention. I am more interested in hearing about how to protect myself from STD's. Remember, I have not been single in over twenty years and it's not that I am even thinking about a relationship right now, but I have to know what is going on out there. Well, my new doctor literally scared the shit out of me. She filled me in on the STD world to such an extent that even kissing a stranger would hardly be worth the risk right now. Don't get me wrong, I am looking forward to having an incredible sex life one day. I know that sex is really important to me, but, after hearing you can get STDs from kissing, oral sex, and everything in between, I think I will take my time!

Anyway, when she was finished examining me, I sat up thinking, *Phew, I'm safe.* And she says (let me add right here that my daughter is leaving in a week for sleep-away camp in Maine), "You have a fibroid cyst/ tumor the size of a grapefruit on your left ovary that I want biopsied ASAP."

Immediately I started feeling around and couldn't understand how anything that big could be inside of me. I'm pretty thin and I thought I would have felt it. Even when I write about that day I still feel sick. Hearing words like that is beyond real. It's like you automatically enter a new world. The anxiety I had was overwhelming. I finally am divorced and moving on and now I have to deal with this . . . alone? As I walked to my car, I looked up in the sky and said, "God, I am begging you. I will never, ever ask for another thing as long as I live if you let me be cancer free for my kids." My ex was not in a great place and I knew my kids needed me, plus all I could think about was my daughter coming home after camp to her mom sick and weak in bed. Would I make it to visiting day? What stage was I in? What hospital would I go to? I had so many questions and unbelievable fears of leaving my kids. A divorce and then your mom has cancer? How could my kids ever handle that?

My MRI had to be done that Saturday; they would not wait. Saturday morning I was taking my daughter to the airport to leave for camp. I had to pretend everything was okay until her plane took off, and then I knew I would break down and lose it. I had to tell my boys I had to have a test but everything was okay. I called my old doctor and told him I needed him and I would not have any procedure done without him in the room. He agreed and told me not to worry about the insurance. I knew no matter what, I was in the best hands I could be in. My doctor and I had to have the best case/worst case talk. They were going to laperscopically do a biopsy while I was in the operating room and try to remove the tumor and possibly part of my ovary, if there were any cancer cells. If they needed to, they might have to do a complete hysterectomy. Best case, it's a fibroid benign tumor and I recover from surgery and I am cancer free.

I left my doctors office, went home and began Googling away. I was reading about my symptoms and already assumed I was in stage three. I began reading about hysterectomies and as soon as I read about hair loss I was done with "the friggin computer that doesn't know anything!" I couldn't read anymore; this was in God's hands. Reading about every possible scenario was only making me think negative thoughts. I just wanted to crawl into bed and make it all go away.

Saturday morning I was going from the airport right to the MRI. I had to drink the barium stuff first thing in the morning and again in a few hours. The whole drive to the airport I held in my tears. It's emotional enough to say good-bye to your daughter for the summer but to have this on top of it was painful. I honestly could not look her in the eye. What would she ever do without me?

I finally got to the hospital and was really scared. I had the nicest male technician who knew I was freaking out. As soon as the MRI was over, I asked him a million questions but they really don't know anything until a radiologist reads the results, which wouldn't be until Monday. It was going to be a very long weekend.

Monday finally came and my doctor called and said it was definitely a mass that needed to be removed, immediately. All I wanted to do at this point was just get it out of my body. I was working so hard on my health. Throughout my divorce, I developed major stomach problems and indigestion and now I was feeling better. I started doing facial acupuncture and I was exercising and eating healthy and preparing for my next life. I knew in my heart that this tumor was from all of the days and months of living in fear and being under enormous stress. I felt so unhealthy before I filed for divorce. I was scared, anxious, and unsure about my future. My ex was so angry I would shake just from any contact. I was finally starting to feel safe again and now this.

Surgery day finally came and while they were prepping me and taking blood and my blood pressure the nurse was speaking to me about the procedure and I honestly didn't hear one word she said. All I knew was that I was about to find out if I had cancer. My grandmother died of ovarian cancer at the age of ninety so it was in the family. As they wheeled me down for surgery, I once again looked up to the sky and reminded God of my three kids and begged Him to spare me, and if he did I would continue to be the best mom I could be. I would try not to let my emotions get the best of me, and I would be a life coach and help other people. The mask went on and I fell asleep quickly.

When I began to wake up, I hesitated to open my eyes. I really didn't want to know what happened. I was either fine, ovary-less with the early stages of menopause invading my body (a symptom of a hysterectomy), or maybe the cancer had already spread. I woke up with my GYN of twenty years, who had been through everything with me: pregnancies, my divorce, everything. He was holding my hand and I finally got up the courage to open my eyes and look at him. He said, "It was the size of a grapefruit and in a really hard place to get to. It was sort of on the side of your ovary."

I'm not even really listening to the details; *just get to the point.* "It was a very bizarre ovarian fibroid benign cyst." I am so out of it I had to think for a minute. Benign is good, right? As tears fell down my face, he looked me in the eye and said, "Now go out there and live your life. Go get 'em!"

I remember that week Patty came to see me at home while I was recuperating. Michael Jackson had just died and we were watching his memorial service and crying our eyes out! My son, by the way, mentioned as he passed by the TV that he had no idea Michael Jackson was black! Anyway, we sat there talking about the *Thriller* days. For us, it was during college. Although I was crying most of the day for Michael's children, I was so relieved mine would be spared the horrible pain of loosing a parent.

After all was said and done, I had to believe that I was one of the lucky ones who was spared and it only meant I have important things to accomplish while I am here on this earth. Now whenever I am having a bad day, or one of my kids is complaining about something unimportant, I can say, "But there are people who have real problems, like cancer, out there." As bad as things are sometimes, someone else is having a much worse day than we are. Things like cancer scares happen for a reason. It's up to us to figure out what the reasons are . . .

BFF'S

I have my foursome—one is from college, one from camp, one from home, and one is blood (I'm sure you realized— my sister). I consider myself pretty lucky to have four great women who I can tell anything to at any time of any day. I call them to cry and to laugh. I love when I make them laugh. It makes me realize my sense of humor is still intact. When going through trauma sometimes you forget to laugh. Anyway, one day one said said to me, "I hope I am in the book!" Yes, I will refer to the girlfriends here and there, but in reality I wanted to say to her, *You are in every page and every sentence because in reality if I didn't have you guys through this time there would be no book, no business, no strong, independent girl that I have become, no great mother I have learned to be.* So yes, you are all in the book.

I am currently in the process of selling my house, which is a huge deal! Not only will it give me complete financial independence, I am moving my kids and me to a new place. Sometimes the thought of packing up all of these memories scares me—what do you do with the wedding album and all the pictures? I think I will put everything in a box so that when my kids are older and ask questions and want to see things, I will have things to show them. It used to make me sad to think about actually doing it, but as the days go on it gets less painful. I feel a real shift in the energy of the house. I feel like my kids and I are just waiting to start fresh, start new, new towels, new energy, new everything. If you really think about it, I am teaching them that it's okay to move on, although we all get scared sometimes.

I need to show them as long as there is love in your life (they have tons!) then things will be okay. Most importantly, Mom is doing okay. There are still times I cry or get angry, but we all know it will pass and besides I believe it's good to show emotions and not keep them bottled up inside, which eventually only causes explosions that cause others pain—been there, lived that! Let's not even go there. Here is another question my friends ask: are you going to put "that part" in the book? I don't really know yet. Sometimes I sit down to write about it, but then I change my mind and don't really feel like getting up the energy to write about all of that. Besides, this is about moving on, and you guys don't want to hear about it, believe me. There are some ugly parts. I had days my friends would beg me to come sleep over so I would not be in the house alone.

When I started negotiating the sale of my house, I was in a panic; it was nerve wracking. The money part of divorce is a bit scary, especially if you were a stay-home mom like me who didn't work and was not involved in the finances. All of a sudden I was trying to write a book, start a business, take care of three kids, and do all of the financial stuff myself. But, like with every other part of divorce, you get stronger more confident and start figuring it all out and it becomes easier. The secret is not to panic. I call my friends crying sometimes and they all say the same thing: "Just get through this part and you will be fine." So the other day I am thinking about moving, picturing my new townhouse, and I start getting excited and I have this gut feeling some lucky-as-hell guy is going to be spending amazing nights in my new bedroom and bathtub with me! So I text one of my tribe mates: "If you build it, they will come!" Holy shit, that's it. I just figured it out. She texts me back saying she is cracking up! I love to use my movie quotes to sum things up!

I JUST HAVEN'T MET YOU YET

I finally got up the nerve to reach out to Mr. X and text and haven't heard anything for five days. I feel as humiliated as Carrie in the *Sexy and the City* movie. Okay, getting dumped on your wedding day is much more serious, but, shit, how do you do that to me? Now what do I do, what do I think, how do I feel? Can you manifest something for a year and it ends like that? Not for me. I just need to give myself recovery time; we all know I always bounce back. I am getting so tired of bouncing around on the emotional roller coaster. My house deal fell through; I am not having a good month. I do remember the Feng Shui lady told me that things are really tough until February— as if she knows anything at all. Who knows? I am getting so sick of all these "predictors." Sometimes they are great, but you can't really rely on anything but your own self.

There's a new song on the radio by Michael Buble: "I Just Haven't Met You Yet." Maybe it's a sign, maybe I have to let all of the old feelings go and start all over again. I am not going to let my heart break again. I can't do it. I would rather be alone. I know I shouldn't feel sorry for myself, but I do. I am good, I love people deeply, and for some reason, except for a few, they haven't been so great to me on the romantic front.

I know it is because I allowed myself to settle a few times too many because I wasn't feeling worthy.

I love my kids so much. Every day they text me to tell me they love me; it's the best feeling. I want everything to be okay for them. I want all three of them to know the deepest love there is someday. It is my wish that they have the very best love, besides mine! I don't know what to make of things right now, but I do know I have to have faith and to believe God is taking care of me. It's hard to even write today, I feel so sad. I thought by now I would be better, and I was. It just got bad again. Maybe one day I will get a surprise and I will understand all of this. I am just hoping that someday some guy is strong enough to help me trust and believe in real love. I know I am sounding negative, but how would you feel right now? I think I will read *Expect a Miracle* tonight. What the hell? Maybe all of this is leading up to something incredibly amazing and I will look back and say it was worth every shitty day and every tear!

I just got an email from Tiffany (as in the little blue box)! Maybe someone is trying to tell me something! I think it's okay to live in dreamland sometimes. I saw two people last night in the city making out in front of Tiffany's and now I just got an email. So what does this mean? My very own Patrick Dempsey *(Sweet Home Alabama)* is going to ask me one day to "pick one out"? Isn't that the key to life—have dreams and hopes and faith? I am so confused. I just called Liz—spiritual psychic, even though according to her this was going to work out. I will see what she has to say about this disaster! Maybe he is going to pull a Richard Gere—I'll take the end of *Pretty Woman* or *An Officer and a Gentleman:* limo or a motorcycle any day. Hey, in both movies the "scared guy who runs away" does end up with the girl, after a lot of pain! Don't a lot of people go through some really tough times and get through them? The saga continues but for now I am finished. I need to pick myself up and put myself back together— especially for those three kids I adore so much!

CINDERELLA

Perfect timing for another soul mate, RI, to show up. OMG he's great sometimes—a real class act. Did I mention him yet? Briefly, we met about six years ago on a weekend I was away with a girlfriend. I was married but not happy and obviously not quite ready to do anything about it because it was six years ago and I haven't even been divorced a year yet. Anyway, I found him on Facebook and emailed, asking him if he was in South Beach six years ago. I figured either he would never remember me or he might recognize my picture. You have to realize it was a long time ago and guys like him I'm sure meet women every day. His response: "Yes, I was in South Beach, how are you?"

It's weird. We speak, email, and text but haven't seen each other. He is the type that would do anything for you, like buy you a five-hundred-dollar bottle of champagne so you don't have to stand at the bar! (True story.) Anyway, when my website was finished I wanted him to see it so I emailed it to him six days ago. I'm driving home from the city Sunday after a sad weekend and I got a message on Facebook: "congrats and the site looks great." I was so happy to hear from him, great timing! I asked when he was coming to visit. What the hell? I was going to be as direct as I want from now on. No more holding back bullshit. It would be fun to see him. And he tells me, "ASAP . . . my kids have swine flu!" Well, my heart stopped. I called but there was no answer so I texted. I was really a little worried for him, but also knew those kids were going to have the best care possible. He's just the kind of guy that would be talking to the doctors and nurses making sure everything was being taken care of, if I was having surgery, he would bring great presents and food! Kind of like a Prince. (Get it? Cinderella.)

RI and I text a little and he disappears as usual, but I guess that's just how it is with texting. You get so into it and then it stops. Yesterday I had a shitty day which you will hear about in the next chapter—mind-blowing stuff! So I decide to take the kids for dinner and afterward I get into bed to watch *Two and a Half Men*—my new favorite show. I love Charlie Sheen in that show so much I just want to jump in the TV. He's funny, has a lot of money, he's cool, cute, so my type. He even has great hair! OMG, does anyone like him really exist who is stable and not in rehab? Anyway, I am watching and laughing—only that show could make me laugh tonight—and I get a text from RI. "How are you and the kids?" Ahh, how sweet is that? What a *mensch* asking about my kids. I melted! Told him we are well but having some tough days but we end up laughing somehow. He said, "I always knew you were strong." So sweet I could get used to this. Then I said, "I thought I was Cinderella". That was our joke when we met because I was always running away from him: I was scared, confused, *married*! I was wondering if he would remember calling me Cinderella, but I took a chance. He texted later, "How funny, you were back then!" How great is that? This is six years later. I texted back, "Never again." He said, "Cinderella has found her Prince. I'm thinking—where, my Prince won't just a text!

I went to sleep in la la land. Cinderella did find her Prince and so will I and he knows it and so do I deep down. Is "Rhode Island" . . . ? No, he can't be. I am not even thinking about it. I am just enjoying the ride for once. He popped in at the right time, maybe he will keep popping up until we see each other. Who knows? I think I am starting to feel a lot better! It's amazing how someone from your past can make you smile (soul mate). Thank you, Facebook!

It's funny how I assumed he might not remember me. It's a lesson for all of us to trust our gut and if you feel like reaching out to someone—do it! You have nothing to lose. Chances are they will be happy to hear from you, and isn't that worth it?

TIS THE HOLIDAY SEASON

I met a BFF from camp yesterday in Long Island for lunch. We had such a great time until I came home with food poisoning and puked all night, like I was back in college! It was scary. Here I was so sick I couldn't even get out of bed. I had towels lined up on the floor, my kids were doing their best, but, for a minute, I thought about calling the police to get me an ambulance, another perk of being single. If you get sick, you are really on your own! My parents were away and I didn't want to wake up my friends. I got through it, fell asleep, and said to myself, "Okay, you made it, you're alive, everyone's okay, no need to have someone here just to hold the garbage pail. You can handle everything that comes your way. These are merely obstacles."

Anyway, I never did hear from Mr. X! My peeps cannot believe it. Come on, who doesn't respond? I laughed about it for a few days, but honestly it hurts like hell. How does someone tell you things like they think they want to marry you and thinking about you makes their heart beat, and then treat you like that? I know it sounds crazy and you are thinking, *Get over it, girl*. The point is life goes on. I am getting Mariah Carey tickets for my daughter and me for New Year's Eve. I thought it would fun to get dressed up and take her to a concert instead of staying home doing nothing. I don't want my boys to be upset if I am alone, so this is better for all of my kids.

It's so hard walking through a store and seeing the holiday dresses. These are the times you have to really be strong and have faith and just know that God will take care of bringing your soul mate to you when it's right. I have to just follow my heart, my dreams, and my intuition and not listen to anybody but myself! It's very important not to listen to other people when it comes to your heart and your feelings. The answers are in your soul. You know what is best for you and nobody else does. I don't believe in going out and looking for love. I will stay true to myself and instead of throwing myself out there, I will continue to work on my body, mind, and spirit so I am ready for that special moment. I know if I keep doing this and growing it will all come to me organically. (No, I am not vegan or anything.) I just believe in good, old-fashioned love and I do believe in faith and God and if this is what gets me through this time in my life, so be it.

After everything that has happened, I have every reason not to believe in love at this point but I do, so much and I am so psyched about it. I have been alone for a while now and I just think it's going to be so amazing to hang out with someone I really dig—someone who makes me laugh! I think the first guy I am attracted to who makes me laugh is going to have me naked in five minutes! Okay, I'm a big talker—maybe ten! Seriously, I can't even imagine. If I meet someone and we have that intense chemistry and sense of humor, who isn't scared and doesn't disappear and stays consistent and has his shit together (I know it's a lot to ask, but as I get happier on my own I get more determined to just wait for the right one—wow.) I waited a long time for it and it's going to be great! What if my book is really made into a movie, like I am hoping? How great would it be to have a movie with a really happy ending that is really my story! It won't be all about sex, but there will be some really *hot* scenes—trust me!

So, if right now I am crying in the car when I hear a love song, so be it. Today I am where I am supposed to be in my life. I have cleared the way for my soul mate, I have taken great care of my kids, and I have weeded out the toxic people and made deeper connections with the good ones. I'm on the right path.

LETTING GO

I'm ready. Something has come over me; there has been a major shift. I decided to let Mr. X go emotionally and it has opened a whole new world for me! I highly recommend it for anyone who is sitting here reading my book, thinking about someone they haven't heard from. You might be reading this book to see if we really end up together because that means the same will happen for you, and it gives you hope. I can honestly say right now I don't know the answer to that, but I do know that I do not fantasize about it anymore, nor do I pray for it. I just pray for the right person to come into my life sooner rather than later. I would not be the girl I am right now sitting on my bed, happy, writing this chapter, if I was in his life now because I would have missed this time alone to recreate myself and my life.

Who knows who will come into my life? Maybe tomorrow I will meet someone amazing, I will be ready now, well, maybe not completely ready but more ready than I have ever been. I just want to stay on the path that I am on and see who I really become. The growth seems to be speeding up lately. I think when you get rid of all the drama and worrying, it's easier to see and feel things. I know it is hard to let go, but do it; let go of all of it; set yourself free! Only you can feel all of this emotional stuff; whoever it is you are obsessing over doesn't feel it. Whether you will end up together is already determined by fate, so why waste your days being upset and worrying about it? It doesn't help. If anything, it makes it worse. Spend the energy and the time on improving yourself and learning to love *you* more than anyone else right now. It's not selfish, it's a must. Love yourself and do "your thing" and just let your life happen.

I let things go and I am doing really well. I honestly hardly ever think about Mr. X. I am writing and working on my business and for the first time in so long I can say I am happy. I have never felt more positive about my future and myself as I do right now. Ironically, it is because no one is in my life or on my mind draining my emotions! The next guy is going to be pretty lucky because he is going to get a whole new me! I already have set the tone. I did it this weekend with "Rhode Island!" Mr. X again has taught me another lesson. (At least he was good for something, other than teaching me what a real "player" is.) The lesson I have learned is to hold onto your own heart until you are really ready to give it to someone who deserves it! Find out *before* you start to fall in love because once those feelings start to come into play you are totally screwed! Once you fall in love, you can't even think straight! When it's mutual, there's nothing better, but when you are being played just to see how far gone you are, the reality becomes painful. Now, to get on with the story or should I say *my story?*

Thanks to Mr. X, I handled "Rhode Island" authentically this weekend! I was a smooth operator. I was at a movie with my newly separated mom and all of a sudden I got a text from Rhode Island saying he is in NYC with his kids! Wow, I can't believe it. He is right here; we haven't been this close in proximity since we met! I am so excited, but the "new" me says, *Think about what to say. He pops in and out your life every month. Take this slow and be smart!* I also know from Facebook he's another player. Okay, I need to think about how I am going to handle Mr. Facebook. So I let him know I am spending the day with my daughter but if I come into the city I will call him—that was honest, I thought. If you are coming to NYC with your kids that means plans were made in advance, so he could have let me know he was coming and I don't want to be another girl on his Facebook, or on anyone's Facebook for that matter. I know he can be seductive and I also know how to handle that one at this point.

Anyway, he continues texting throughout the weekend. It was pretty exciting, I must admit. Sometimes it seems the harder you play hard to get, the more you hear from them! I don't want to be a game player just because he is. I have worked too hard to be an honest, authentic person, so I need to let him know how I want to be treated. So I let him know to call me in advance next time. He says, "Absolutely, I will definitely do that!" I did it. I set him up to see if he is a man of his word. He's very Michael Buble to me. He always reminded me of him. I like when he comments on my photos on Facebook. I think it's hot. I wonder if we ever really have this weekend I have going in my mind: great hotel, romantic sexy dinner, fun shopping during the day. Who knows? We will have to see if "Rhode Island" really has it in him. At least I am now in control of my own game; it feels great to be on this side for once.

I think this is the secret: to be so smart that you outsmart the guy by just being confident and knowing what you want. I set the tone with him: if you want to see me, call me in advance, end of story . . . beginning of my new story.

Here is a blog I wrote for my website on June 7, 2010.

Cinderella is alive and well!

Years ago RI called me Cinderella because I was running away from my heart and myself. At the time I really didn't understand how going against your heart could affect your life. I thought I was doing the right thing by listening to my head. It took me about five years to realize, through some major life changes, that listening to your heart is the only way to go. Listening to your heart means being your authentic self and living against that causes pain, sadness, and fear, indigestion, sickness, anxiety, etc. Get the point?

Today I feel like Cinderella, again. I have been packing boxes and cleaning out drawers, closets, three kids' rooms, everything that has accumulated over the last twelve years. I took a break to do my five-mile run today (no matter what—make time for your health, otherwise you can't think with a clear head). On my run, for some reason Cinderella came to my mind. I realized that I am very similar to her in that I have worked hard raising my kids with all that I have gone through, I have spent the last two weekends packing my house all by myself and just like her never complained or even asked for help. I put music on in the house and just whistled a happy tune! Yes, there were hours when I cried as I looked at old pictures of my kids, but I found happiness knowing we are moving on to new home and a new life. It takes a lot to get three kids and yourself to a new place but I look forward to it.

As I ran today I thought about Cinderella and how even though she spent her days working hard and being mistreated, she was still hopeful and still true to who she was. Look what happened to her—the prince spotted her, out of all the women at the ball. She had a dress made from scratch . . . and you all know the rest of the story. The prince came looking for her—not vice versa! She did not go looking for a man, he came to her.

Yes, I do believe in fairytales, especially this one. I believe if you go about your business, work hard, and maintain your integrity, that your dreams will come true. It has nothing to do with going out and looking. I feel so good knowing what I have accomplished this year with my personal life as well as my career that I know that if I stay on this path, everything will work out the way I always dreamed it would. I know I will have that moment when . . . someone will come along with the shoe that fits perfectly!

I know this because I am happy just being me. Yes, a prince will come, but not to complete you nor make you happy—he will appear as a result of your happiness. He will appear and be drawn to your energy and happiness and want to turn Cinderella into a princess!

WHAT IF

It's that time of year again, the time when I don't know whether to laugh or cry. I feel like everyone is going away on fun vacations, like I used to do. Growing up we never stayed home. We always went skiing to Colorado. I think it was the only time my family ever really spoke to each other. Anyway, until I sell my house, money is tied up and Drew has basketball, so I have legitimate excuses for not being on the beach or skiing. Where would I go anyway? This time of the year is so family oriented. I think that is why it is so hard. It would not be easy to be at a hotel packed with families right now. I think my kids are better off being home with me. Sometimes you feel like such an outsider when you see happy families. Although I know a lot of them are functioning at the "let's pretend we're happy" mode. I still think it's better to be in the lonely stage for now and even though I crave a loving relationship, I know deep down that this is the only way to get there: be alone now so I can celebrate later. Kathy Freston even says to go ahead and throw a party for what you know is coming! Okay, I won't go that far, but I have to go there in my mind; it will keep things in perspective. I have to realize I am one of the lucky ones for not choosing to stay in a mediocre relationship. I am on my way to great love. I am one of the rare people, although maybe there are more than I think, who still believes in a magical kind of love. I really do believe I am Cinderella and that my Prince will find me somehow. I just need to maintain my pride and stick to what I believe, even though I might be a little different from most people. This is who I am.

Sometimes it's hard to understand where people are coming from. "Rhode Island" wanted to see me when he was in New York two weeks ago, but I haven't heard from him. Is this what Kathy Freston means by, *if you see signs of old patterns (Mr. X), just walk away and save yourself the heartache*? I do have to think about myself. I want someone stable and who is emotionally strong. I want to cry on a set of big, strong shoulders and feel secure and protected, and then I want him to make me laugh so hard I cry. Is that too much to ask? How do I get there when the men in my life are just so afraid? I guess we will have to find out as the book and my life continue.

We have to realize there is always another perspective on things. The other night I was talking to a single guy friend, about Mr. X. He said something that has stuck in my mind for days: "What if you really hurt him?" By what, not leaving my marriage so quickly? I had to make sure I was making the right decision for myself. You can never ever make life-changing decisions for anyone but yourself.

I have to live in reality now and learn to love my life and do what is best for my kids and me. Even though I have some great friends and family members, the truth is all you really have is you and your kids; that is who is there for you and with you 24/7. No one else, so cherish that.

You never really feel as divorced as you do around the holidays. I am trying to make it as pleasant as I can for all of us, but in reality it sucks. It sucks not to buy a special gift for someone, it sucks not be on vacation with someone, it sucks knowing there is no one to kiss on New Year's Eve. But, like I said, it's worse to be in something that isn't right that is causing you pain and not allowing you to be your real self. I guess it sucks both ways, until that one special day . . . when you are so grateful for getting through the "sucks" part because you look at what it brought you.

There is always the hope and the "what ifs . . ." What if my soul mate is getting his life together and he is right now trying to make his way to me? It's possible, anything is. What if . . . doesn't that sound more romantic than being sad? I love romance! We have to think about the "what ifs." We have to believe that something great is on the way. We have to get ready for it, that is what this time is all about: getting ready for that moment in time that is going to change everything. That moment when we think, *That last year wasn't that bad. I would do it again in a heartbeat . . . for what I have now."*

It's not only about thinking about the future because we need to live in the moment and be present right here and now for our children's sake and our own. We don't want to be one of those people living unconsciously. Our children will suffer from that. We have to stay in the moment and be happy for each day, and be happy we are aware of life around us and not just waiting, even though a part of us really is. We have to keep working on other parts of ourselves as we keep growing and changing. New possibilities will present themselves and who knows, maybe the soul mate you dream about today will be a totally different person tomorrow because you are changing and you want that person to come into your life at exactly the right time. So, like me, take the time to figure out what you really want and figure out who you really are. I feel like I have waited a million days already, so what's another million? It's worth the wait because I am learning to like myself more and more.

"IT'S COMPLICATED"

It is December 26 and there are five more days until New Year's Eve. Although I am alone, I plan to spend it eating great food and watching a movie. And yes, I still have sadness inside me and have those loneliness pangs every once in a while. It's a feeling I get in my stomach for a few seconds when I am sad, but it goes away as fast as it comes. My CD of the week is Alicia Keys. There are a few songs about "honest pain," the kind you have when you can admit how much you love and miss someone even though he won't return your call or anything. Yes, I still do miss Mr. X, but, like Alicia Keys says, I can wait another million days if I have to! There is a very sad part of me, but there is also a side of me that is filled with hope. I know the girl I am and I know what I want as far as love goes, and I know somehow, someway, it will come.

I know I haven't written about my parents' situation so here goes, short and sweet. After fifty years of marriage, they are splitting up. I must say, as bad as I feel for my parents, I knew all along their marriage wasn't right. I have to be happy for anyone who, like me, decided to leave the comfort zone and take another route in life. Some people think they can go on forever living in that mediocrity, that day-to-day "being there" but not *being* there. When you are in your marriage just to stay married, for some it works, but for others who need and want something so much better for themselves, for those of us who need to grow, it doesn't really work. It becomes too painful not to be yourself. It becomes too painful to exist without love and passion. My heart bleeds for those who do not "get it," for those who will always be too afraid to be on their own because they will never know what it is like to love themselves and ultimately to truly love someone else.

I still have my moments when I am crying or angry at things that have happened in my life, but, all in all, I did what I had to do to: change them and live an authentic life. If I wasn't in this position myself, maybe I wouldn't understand my parents. If this happened a long time ago, things would be different. I might really resent my parents for splitting up, but deep down in my heart I know what it is like to be in a marriage that leaves you feeling lonely and passionless, one where you can't really be yourself because the other person is too afraid for you to change. Believing there is someone out there who will understand who you are and allow and honor your growth, and grow with you, is worth taking chances for.

Until that day, just have the faith and integrity to stand on your own two feet and to teach your children what love and strength is all about. Even though divorce is devastating and painful for kids, it also teaches about courage and love and understanding and it shows our kids that the love we have for them is unconditional—that no matter what or where we are, we love our kids every minute of every day. Marriage and relationships change sometimes but the relationships we have with our kids remains the same forever and ever. I might not have anyone to lie in bed with right now, but the hugs from my kids and the "love u" texts I get every day are worth more to me today than having ten guys in my bed.

I do love both of my parents and know they love me. Part of me wishes this didn't happen because I am a little bit fragile right now and although their marriage wasn't right, they were stability for me. I wish things could have been different for me and my brother and sister growing up, as I am sure many of you reading this book can relate to. So many of us are divorced, I believe, because we don't want to be like our parents. We want more out of our marriages and we aren't accepting things the way that they did. Marriage is not a life sentence to us—at least not to me. It is a commitment to be your best self for your spouse. Whether I choose to get married again or not—I probably will but this time it will be so much deeper; this time it will not be about having kids and buying a house, etc.; this time it will be about love and growth and watching each other get to places we only dream about. It will be about two people who have probably been through one divorce already and have gone through this transformation stage where they have reinvented themselves and the possibilities will be endless. You get to a point where you start to just "know" your soul mate is out there and it is just a matter of time until your worlds collide.

I have had this vision of myself sitting at the head of a long table with my new husband, soul mate, at the other end. There are older kids filling the seats alongside us and everyone is laughing and having fun. It is a holiday dinner. I'm not sure which one, but there is no tension. Everyone is relaxed and I am watching my kids, and I look straight ahead and the love of my life is telling one of his funny stories and I am just staring at him, not even listening. I am teary eyed and in awe of this man who finally found me, who I adore, who adores me every day. He's in the middle of the story (loves himself and loves making people laugh) and he looks at me for a second and sees tears in my eyes and smiles at me with a tear in his eye as well. We both don't need to say a word. He will continue with the funny story and I will continue to stare at him knowing later I will get into bed with him and never, ever be lonely again. So all of these days and nights for now are okay because I know what is coming. I can feel it in all my soul, and that's what living an authentic life is all about: being true to yourself and what you really want. I know that my kids know that something great is coming. I am sure they wish it to be sooner rather than later, but I also want them to know I am okay on my own. That's the reason I will be okay when he arrives.

On that note, I am going to see Alec Baldwin's new movie *It's Complicated* tonight. He is so Mr. X to me. He's funny and sexy as hell. Kathy Freston says when you get impatient waiting, go to a movie. I think it's the perfect night!

"DARKNESS IS PART OF THE PLAN"

I made it! I got through the brutal holidays. And I had to spend them without having my dad around. Phew . . . But through it all, I can't help believing that the amazing love of my life will someday arrive and I will be better and stronger than ever. Although I can't wait, I will be patient because, after going through this, I will appreciate it even more . . . and choose the most perfect mate for me. Notice I said, "for me." Nobody is perfect. We all have our faults *and* we all have suffered on some level. It's the ones who can get past it that will turn out the best! The ones who stay angry and resentful have no shot at true love, only a shot at being with someone just as "negative."

A few days ago my daily Kabbalah email said, "Darkness is part of the plan." I was so happy to get that one! It is a reminder to me, and everyone for that matter, that we all go through our painful moments but there is a reason for it. It is all just a part of the plan that God has for us. Shit, does that statement say it all. How dark do things have to get? I have just added my parents' break up to my list this year. I think I have had more heartache this year than most people have in ten! I know some people would not be functioning without therapy, but I have come to realize that what helps me the most is helping others through their pain and giving great "advice"—love it! So instead of talking to a therapist and analyzing my life to death, I am writing articles for my coaching business and writing this book to help whoever is reading it.

I think I am beginning to feel a little less "divorced" and a little more normal. I love the line in the movie *It's Complicated* when Meryl Streep says it takes at least two years to feel "normal" again. Well said! It's so true. I am starting to look at myself as a person, not as a single parent. What a tough thing it is to be the only parent in the house with two teenage boys and a daughter turning thirteen! Scary at times, but honestly not so bad. I think I am doing a great job. When you are close to your kids, and single, they see your ups and downs and have to learn a new way to get through it all. They know even if I am sad that in a few hours I will be laughing again. They are learning some great lessons. Life might really suck sometimes, but there is always the next hour, the next day.

Another great line in the movie is when Steve Martin tells Meryl Streep that the thing he loves about her is "her age." How romantic and cool is that? I am so tired of hearing people say that guys in their forties only want girls in their thirties! Not *all* of them, not the ones who have evolved and care more about the relationship than their own egos. How silly did Alec Baldwin look in that fertility clinic? He had so much more fun hanging out with his ex-wife. How great was it when they got stoned? Who wants to do that with a thirty-year-old? What do you laugh about?

One more thing to comment on: Susan Sarandon and Tim Robbins' recent split. Sad, but all I kept thinking about when I saw a picture of her was how hot she looks at age sixty! Does she convey the meaning of "sexy" or what? It just goes to show that it doesn't matter how old you are, it matters how you feel about yourself. People will feel about you the same way you feel about yourself. Rumor has it she is with a much younger guy— I think a younger guy who likes older women is hot if they can handle a mature relationship! I love Ashton and Demi. Come on, she has never looked better. They adore each other and they let you know it. I think a man who loves his woman is sexy as hell. The ones who are always complaining and trying to get away from their mates are miserable and look it! When they put down the woman they are with, they are announcing their own insecurities. If you really feel that way about her, then why are you with her? I think it is just about the way you really feel about yourself. The same holds true for women who constantly put down their men. What does that really say about you? I wish I could start a movement and be Dr. Love! I so want everyone to be in love. We spend more time out of it than in it. If there is no one to be in love with, at the moment, find someone. Better yet, be in love with yourself. You're bound to attract the right one at the right time. Loving yourself makes you radiant and desirable, plus it feels pretty damn good!

Instead of feeling sorry for yourself for being alone (this is what helped me the most), anticipate, dream, manifest, meditate, and think about how great it will be when you finally meet your soulmate. Get so specific about it that you feel his hands in yours: you smell him as he kisses your neck, picture him lying next to you as you turn the light out to go to sleep. While you're making dinner, think about how happy he will be when he finally sits down to hang out with you tonight. Go there! Don't waste all of those hours thinking about how shitty it is to be alone, or how long it's been since you had sex. All of that is a big, fat waste of time. What's the point? It only shows the universe that you are not ready! Show it that you are and that you can't wait. Believe in your soul that it's taking so long because it is going to be that much better. You and your soul mate have to get to the perfect place separately so you can find each other at the perfect moment.

BEFORE THERE WAS . . . MATCH.COM

I know I may seem old-fashioned, but my feeling (that I will prove true) is that for thousands and thousands of years before JDate, Match.com, or F-ckbook came along, people were falling in love every day. Yes, I am experimenting with online dating and writing blogs about the experience, and yes, I know technology is changing and we must keep up with the times, but who is to say what will be ten years from now? Maybe more of us will go back to the old-fashioned way of dating: courting. How great would it be to be Audrey Hepburn in *Breakfast at Tiffany's*? She was so terrified of love and so vulnerable but found a man who wouldn't let her go! How about *The Notebook*—killer or what? One of the greatest love stories as far as I'm concerned! That reunion kiss! And that painting studio he built for when she came back? He manifested and it worked. How happy was she to paint naked on the balcony—so happy and alive! Yes, I know these are movies, but we all know someone who has a great story to tell. I am determined to be one of them. Have you ever read the Sunday Styles section of the *New York Times?* My dream is to be on the back page one day.

I believe you have to create your story in your head and let it come to life. What you think will happen . . . will. It may take some time, and the time can be really painful, but you have to keep believing and going to your dreams in your mind. Like I always say—there is a reason for the pain. I still believe that there is some grand plan for all of us, we all just have to wait our turn. Meanwhile, keep your energy pure so new people can find you.

THE LOVE YOU ARE LOOKING
FOR IS LOOKING FOR YOU

I am getting so much clearer and better on my own. I am much more relaxed. I am finding inner peace and happiness. I lost some "stress" weight and I am feeling really good. I've been getting really into Debbie Ford's work. She has a great website with meditations. I will get more into that soon.

Alot of the books I read are so hung up on "playing it cool." I think if you are thinking about someone, letting him know is cooler. No, I will not throw myself at anyone, but once every month or so, if the spirit moves me, then so what? In a way, Mr. X is still my muse, he is still my catalyst, he is still getting me to where it is I am supposed to be going. The point is I am turning into the girl I wanted to be for so long and he started me on this journey.

It is mind boggling to me that after twenty years of marriage and three kids, my ex and I can't even have a conversation—even though we slept in the same bed for that long. They say if you didn't have good communication when you were married, forget about when you are divorced! I think the worst part about my divorce is that we became strangers overnight. There are some moments when, even after everything you have been through, you will be walking down the hall to go to bed, or waking up on a Sunday morning and you feel a pang of missing the old days, and it can hurt for a few minutes, a part of your life has died, but as you go through the day you remember why you are no longer together, you are two different people now. We are not the same as we were when we were twenty-five.

The lucky couples grow together; the not so lucky ones have to go through major growth changes, grief, anger, and sadness until their lives are once again put back together. We can't change who we are nor can we live in skin that does not feel comfortable to us. Although so many people do, it is toxic. They end up getting physically ill and that is so sad to me. People would rather live that way than take chances and move through the fear and come out on the other side. So many people do not even know what I am talking about, they just pretend and stay in their safety zone. I don't know. I just wish we could all be ourselves and say what we really want to say and do what we really want to do. It would be so much easier than hiding behind our fears. Sometimes I sit here reading advice from relationship experts about "playing the game" and I get tired just reading it. It's so much easier to just be you: if it works it works, if not just keep being yourself for the next one, eventually I think it will all come together.

In the movie *He's Just Not That into You,* she was so vulnerable and naïve and look what happened—Justin Long ended up falling for her because she was so real. Don't we all, at the end of the day, just want to be comfortable with our soul mates and be ourselves? There has to be someone out there who is just right for you, for me, for everyone, but how will we ever know if we are too busy pretending we are someone else? Although it gets really lonely at times, I feel so relieved to just be myself, you have no idea.

Debbie Ford has a great quote she uses: "The love you are looking for is looking for you." Doesn't that just change your whole belief system? That is my new mantra. You are not the only one thinking about that amazing connection. Obviously your future soul mate is as well. I get the goose bumps thinking about it. Hi, soul mate! Love you already!

WHEN IT HURTS . . . CRY!

Here is the best piece of advice I am ever going to give you: when it hurts, cry. Don't fight the feeling by trying to hold it in because it will only keep coming back. As soon as you get that lonely pang or sad feeling, excuse yourself and cry those eyes out! Why? Because, trust me on this, you will feel so much better after you do. When you hold those feelings in, they get stronger and stronger and start to make you feel sick. To be perfectly honest, weekends are not that easy. I have no desire to hang out in bars and I am not thirty or even forty for that matter. I still have a young spirit, but I haven't really figured out what to do with it. Things are even changing now with my middle child. He is turning seventeen and I know he knows I am cool but lately he will do anything he can to let me know I am not. We laugh because I know it is a phase.

My other son just texted me to see who I am watching football with—my kids know I like to watch—and I had to say, "Myself." Well, the tears just poured and poured. I hate telling them when I am alone. I tell my kids that I am okay when I am by myself and that is so important for anyone single with kids who is reading this. Yes, it is hard for the kids to see their parents alone, but what is far worse is for them thinking their parents are not happy. No matter what happens in life, it is up to us parents to show our children that life still goes on and nothing can ever change that. I tell my kids all the time, "Divorce stinks but it isn't cancer and it isn't death." "we are all responsible for our own happiness".

I go through different emotions every hour. When I am feeling really sad, I cry and then the optimist in me starts to push away the sadness and says, "It's coming, there is something really wonderful coming." I really believe it and that is the best part of my day. Those few moments when I am really filled with hope, and I can almost feel myself in a new life. A life where I know I have someone's arms to lie in every night, no matter what the day was like. A life where my work is really helping other people and I am making money for my kids. A life where I feel loved and confident and feel like I am finally living my purpose. A life where I can sit on a beach and look out into the waves and think about all I had to go through in order to get to this beautiful place. I don't really understand why "darkness is part of the plan" or why we all have to go through so much before we get to the other side. I just know that thinking about the other side is getting me there.

I am sitting here watching the Jets game and they just announced that the Jet who just caught the ball and scored a touchdown (it's a really big game) suffered a major loss this week—his forty-seven-year-old dad died. I think, *And here is this kid playing in probably the biggest game of his career and he is scoring!* It's amazing how some people rise to the occasion. It makes me realize I do too. Everyone has their own setbacks and challenges, which is what makes us who we are . . . and better yet, who we will be.

EMOTIONALLY AVAILABLE . . .
OR AS I LIKE TO SAY *READY*

I found this amazing letter online. Debbie Ford's sister Arielle Ford has a website and she posted it today. When you read it, you will know it is so me! I made two copies of it right away and put one on my wish board and one next to my bed. After I read it, I was in such a good mood I lit my candles and got into the bathtub and just started talking to myself and had this amazing idea to have a "bathtime podcast" on my website so I can talk to you guys from my bathtub at night. I quickly called my publicist and told her about it—it can be like Run DMC on Run's House! She told me after I have been in business for as long as him!

I felt so positive today and I felt really pretty. It's unbelievable how your mind-set really affects your looks. I had on the same makeup and everything but I was really digging myself, even my skin looked really young and healthy! The best part is that my daughter, who is really into watching *Desperate Housewives* reruns, told me I look like Teri Hatcher! I was jumping up and down, Googling pictures of her, and hugging my daughter. Even she noticed a change in me tonight. I wish I could bottle this feeling and drink it on the not as great days. I guess you can't appreciate the good stuff if you don't have some of the bad. Here is my favorite letter–

Dear One,

Everyone longs to give themselves completely to someone, to have a deep soul relationship with another, to be loved thoroughly and exclusively, but I say "NO," not until you are satisfied, fulfilled and content with being alone, with giving yourself totally and reservedly to Me, will you be ready to have the intensely personal unique relationship that I planned for you. You will never be united with anyone or anything else until you are united with Me. I want you to stop planning, stop wishing, and start allowing Me to give you the most thrilling plan in existence—one that you cannot even imagine. I want you to have the best. Please, allow me to bring it to you.

You must keep watching Me expecting the greatest of things. Keep experiencing the satisfaction that I AM. Keep listening and learning the things that I will tell you. Just wait. That's all. Don't be anxious. Don't worry. Don't look around at the things other have or that I have given them. Don't look at the things you think you want. Just keep looking up to me or you will miss what I want to show you. And then, when you are ready, I will surprise you with a love far more wonderful than any you dreamed of.

You see, until you are ready and until the one I have for you is ready (I am working even at this moment to have you both ready at the same time), until you are both satisfied exclusively with Me and the life I have prepared for you, you won't be able to experience the love that exemplifies your relationship with Me. This is Perfect Love.

And dear one, I want you to have this most wonderful love. I want to see in the flesh a picture of your relationship with me, and to enjoy materially and concretely the everlasting union of beauty,

perfection and love that I offer. Know that I love you utterly.
Believe it and be satisfied.

Love,
God

I love this letter! It made me refocus my thoughts. It made me realize that my wish wall which has lists of qualities I want my soul mate to have, pictures of dresses I want to wear with him, and couples I admire—Paul Newman and Joanne Woodward, Demi Moore and Ashton, Penelope and Xavier, Cindy and Rande Gerber, Michelle Pfeifer and David Kelly, Warren Beatty and Annette Bening—was missing something. I forgot "emotionally available!" Maybe I never realized it because I really wasn't ready until now. What if Mr. X could still have all of the qualities but *also* be emotionally ready—be fun, funny, romantic, sexy and loyal but also call me whenever he thinks of me, surprise me with visits, miss me when he's not with me, texts me one thousand times a day, and call me at night for hour-long miss-you-talks. Was I not thinking, was I really willing to spend my time dreaming about all of this, if he would never be emotionally stable? Don't I want to be able to cry on someone else's shoulder after all of these months alone? Do I ever want to be in the hospital again with no one holding my hand? No, I want strength and stability and emotional support. I want to end my day in bed with someone I look up to and adore, *not* someone I had to practically beg for. What's the point in getting the "prize" if you're going to spend half the week crying and worrying? I have said this from the beginning of my "single life" and I will keep saying it: he will appear at the right time and at the right place. Worrying will only give me reasons for Botox. To stay young and pretty, I have to stop worrying and just look forward to it with all of my heart, which is getting so big that I think it's going to burst if I don't get to love someone soon!

I do know that the next guy I meet who doesn't call when he says he will and who texts instead of calling, or who pops in and out every few weeks or months, is not emotionally stable and is not worthy of my love, my love is *huge*. The next one is so lucky. I now really believe that and that took a long time. All of the work I have done to get to a better place will not be destroyed ever by a guy who is not emotionally stable. They are hurtful, even if they don't mean to be.

So I think about the letter all the time now. Whether it was really written by God or not, the point is someone had enough insight to post it. We all have to believe in our own God and our own destinies.

"I'M NOT GONNA TELL YOU
WHAT YOU WANNA HEAR"

I am going to take you back in time a little bit. I met with my publicist today, who I love like a sister. We are a generation apart but I have such respect for her and her work. Anyway, we started to tell each other stories about things that have happened to us and I went into a story about Mr. X that I really had forgotten about until now. After I told her, we decided it had to be the next chapter.

To give you a brief introduction, for my forty-fifth birthday I had my boobs done! It was totally against my husbands wishes, but I finally decided my body, my decision. I waited many more years than I wanted to because whenever I brought it up, we ended up having a fight. Finally I was fed up. I love my body and after having three kids I wanted to have great boobs again. End of story.

My sister-in-law was opening a store in LA at the time and really wanted either me or my husband to come for the opening. Guess who went just days out of surgery? First night there, I was in her apartment and her friend came over to blow-dry my hair because, even though I took a chance and flew to LA, I wasn't able to lift my arms. I washed my hair in the sink and stood up and started to feel pain in my boob and just assumed I overdid it a little bit with all of the traveling. My husband was very distant at the time and was still angry about the surgery *(Get over it and enjoy that I have these great boobs* was my feeling). Plus, every time I called him, he just complained about watching the kids. Okay, it's not like I am at Canyon Ranch—and even if I was, I deserved better.

Meanwhile, I noticed my boob was starting to really bleed. I called my sister-in-law and said, "Take me to the hospital." Mr. X calls and I tell him what's happening and he says, "Let me know when you are okay." Anyway, my sister-in-law and her guy friend come get me. I am so sick by now I can't even get dressed. We head to UCLA emergency room; I am wearing nothing but a short, black, silk robe. I am in such pain I am literally holding my boob. I didn't even care that this friend of hers is seeing me barely dressed—that's how much pain I am in. I am picturing my boob exploding in UCLA hospital! We get to the emergency room and I am literally screaming from the pain but have to sit and wait in the crowded waiting room.

I was screaming and in so much pain they had to put me in a room and hook me up to a morphine pump! Mind you, there are heart attack patients, terminally ill patients—I mean this is UCLA emergency room at night, and here I am flipping out and screaming in my robe holding my boob. Now I can almost laugh but it was so awful, worse than giving birth to my first child who was frank breach—butt first, folded in half with no epidural! I stayed this way from 11:00 p.m. to 5:00 a.m. when the plastic surgeon finally showed up. Cute one I might add; it's LA. Finally he takes one look at my boob and cancels his surgeries and says, "You are an emergency!" I said, "Ya' think? Where have you been?"

I was taken directly to the operating room. Let me just say that I thought I entered paradise. Not only was I finally getting help, but the anesthesiologist was in a bandana blasting the Rolling Stones in the ER . . . As he put the mask on me to put me to sleep he said, "You poor thing, you're going to be okay." I looked into his gorgeous face and thought, *Wow, there are compassionate, adorable men out there . . . Thank God!"*

I woke up hours later with one implant in and one out! I was flipping out. I don't mean any disrespect, but I can only imagine what women with breast cancer must go through when they have to wake up from surgery with one or two breasts removed. Because of this experience, I now think about these women in a whole new light. Anyway, the doctor tells me I was lucky they operated when they did, because I had a massive infection and they removed two pints of blood—that's how blown up that boob was! All I want to know was "When is the implant going back in." He says, "Six months." What? It's March, summer is coming what am I supposed to do with one boob? It's bathing suit season and I am supposed to have my hot little body back, not be on the beach with one boob!

To make a long story short, I called my New York surgeon who after scolding me for being in LA so soon tells me if I can make it home in seven days, she can put it back in, otherwise it's six months. I am hooked up to antibiotics, morphine, and God know what else, but I am sure you already know I am definitely flying to New York in seven days. I was so tired and weak and to top it off my husband was still having a hard time being compassionate . . . to put it nicely.

Mr. X called to see how I was and I just wanted to cry. I told him I was so out of it and tired and I had to sleep and he said, "Sweet dreams." I slept like a baby the rest of the day with that cell phone glued to my hand. I laid in that bed for four days with no flowers, not a balloon, not a thing from my husband. I decided then that I wasn't in the best relationship. I was afraid that someday I would be in the hospital really sick and my husband would not be there emotionally (again), unless of course I had a legitimate illness that he approved of.

I began asking myself what I was really doing. I knew I needed more. Shit, I had been there for this man for twenty years of my life and for once I needed him to show up and he couldn't. I managed to fly home in time, after my plane stopped in Houston. (My husband didn't book a direct flight to New York and I could hardly walk.) I had to get around the airport in a wheelchair; I couldn't even lift my bag. I finally landed in New York but didn't feel comfortable being home. Something had changed . . . I just didn't know at that moment that it was changing forever.

When I got back home I was not well enough to do anything, especially not file for divorce. You have to be really sure before you change your children's lives, yours, and your husbands forever. More time went on. We even went on a trip to Telluride—my marriage counselor and I decided it would be the last try. I tried, but after LA it was never the same. I realized I wanted and needed more than my husband could even understand. We were not the same; I started to realize there is another depth of love that I wanted, that I needed, that I would be okay giving to myself until "the right one" came along. I could no longer stay in a marriage for my husbands sake. My life had to be about what I needed and me. Some might call it selfish but I knew he blocked out so much and probably could have gone on forever, but I knew I could not be a good mom, sister, daughter, or friend if I stayed in this marriage. It's so painful to know you are breaking someone's heart, but I kept trying to make my husband understand and go to therapy but there was no change. I was growing at a rapid rate and could not stop. It was too painful to try to stop. I needed to be me, and I needed the freedom to be a whole person again. I could not bear to be put down anymore for the things that mattered to me. I don't think it's fair to my children or my ex to go any further into the issues. However, I do know now that when someone is not really happy on the inside, they take it out on the ones they are closest to and even tend to be abusive. Some people get the help they need and others stay in denial, blaming the one who wants out.

So here I sit, the eve before my one-year divorce anniversary, and yes, it still hurts. It is still hard, but staying would have been harder. I do believe things work out for everyone, even though it's hard to see that when you are in the middle of all the drama. I believe there is a forever kind of love for everyone, no matter when it starts. Sometimes it can be a first marriage that lasts forever and sometimes it's the second one. Let's not even discuss a third one! I know after going through all of this that my next marriage will be the "forever" one. It took me years of working on my "stuff" and I still am and I will continue with the next love of my life . . . I know that no one can stop me. I cannot stop my journey; I can only invite people to join me on it. There might be heartbreak, and I am sure there will be intense joy, but it is *my* journey and my path and my choices. I have finally learned to love myself enough to know how I want to be loved and how I want to love and live.

In case you were wondering why I named this chapter "I'm Not Gonna Tell You What You Wanna Hear," around this time Mr. X said that to me. We never finished the conversation and to this day, we still haven't. Sometimes we don't get the answers we need; but, sometimes we have to have our own closure so we can move on.

WHAT I KNOW

Wow! I am really going to be an excellent Lifestyle Coach! I am doing this program that I made up myself. It is a combination of books, coaching, meditations, etc. It is my version and it is working. I have not woken up sad once this week! If those damn hormones mess this up next week, I am going to be really pissed. Anyway, I have changed my energy significantly. My parents are going through a real, full-fledged, lawyers and all divorce, and I am still okay. I know I had to travel on my own road to get here, and there have been tough as hell days and I am sure there will be more, but wow, when you start to see the light, it is mind blowing. I am really pretty lucky right now; I have everything I need to have an amazing second half of my life! I am single and for the first time it feels really good! I have created the life for myself that is going to bring me the greatest love story ever! It no longer matters to me when, where, and why. I just know it is coming and I am going to be so ready.

When you change your inner energy, the world changes with you. I know it sounds like self-help bullshit, but it is so not. If you don't believe me then either try it for yourself or stay miserable for the rest of your life. It's really a simple choice. I am good when it comes to intuition. For example, I have been telling my friends to eat dark chocolate for years. Yesterday I had such an "ah ha" moment. I walk into CVS and there it is: Dark Chocolate Reese's! Yay! And this I could not believe: Godiva at CVS. No more making excuses to go to the mall! Now most people would say, "No big deal," but I knew when I walked out of the store that I am onto big things, my intuition is right on target. I have worked so hard to become a Lifestyle Coach. On the West Coast coaching is huge, but here in New York everyone is just starting to catch on.

Right now everyone is so worried about the economy, which stinks! But I know this is all going to pass. It's a perk of being a positive person. I know the future is bright for all of us. I know we have all learned a huge lesson. I know that tapping out the credit cards will only lead to this again, I know that we are all starting to eat healthy and think about what we are doing to our bodies, I know we are closer to our kids than our parents were to us. I know that we are not "sticking it out" in mediocre marriages. I know we are going to live longer than the generation before us. I believe the reason so many people get cancer is stress related. I know there is a really deep kind of love if you are willing to go there. I know that if you fear love you will never have it. I know my kids will be okay because I am stronger than the women in my family before me. I know it's really important to laugh every day and to be with someone who not only agrees but who makes you laugh. I know what it feels like to have a guy say and think you are gorgeous, I know that if I died tomorrow I have left this book for my kids to read. I know I have taught them more this year than any other. I know how to change my life and I know I will change many others along the way. I know that I really do have a gift to share with not only the future soul mates or soul mate in my life but with my friends, family, people reading this book, and future clients.

How do I know all of that? I have learned to clear my mind and open myself up to all of life's possibilities. I will always have me and I am really starting to love me and just want to keep going and going and growing and growing and knowing and knowing.

I have started another ritual, I pray every night and every morning. Sometimes it's that the ex and I can be friends one day. I pray both of my parents will find true happiness. I pray that my kids know real love one day. I always end with a prayer for Mr. X—that he can get past his pain and really grow the same way I have so that he can come to me one day soon (whoever he is). I have realized lately I will not be able to have a causal thing with him. It would have to be all or nothing. I don't mean we have to get married. I mean it would have to be a committed relationship to see how far it can go. I don't know if God thinks I am ready for that. Maybe he wants me to be with other men first. Otherwise He would have brought him to me by now. There is something that needs to be done besides my transformation that I don't know about yet. I just know that's why he's not here . . . yet. He needs to be ready too. I am not going to fix anyone. They need to be at the right place in their lives so we can move on together and not spend our days trying to fix what's broken . . .

Do you see a major difference in my tone lately? I will tell you what I am doing besides praying. I have been manifesting. I spend time manifesting on my soulmate, my career and my body. I am also reading a great book called *Finding Your Half Orange*. The author, Amy Spencer, is living my life. She is from New York and now lives in Venice with her "half orange." Anyway, since I have been manifesting so much I have started to lose these stubborn eight pounds that appeared out of nowhere.

RI popped back into my life today! I was getting out of my meditative, candlelit bath, and *ping*—a text: "Hello Gorgeous, just left you a message on Facebook." OMG to hear, or should I say to read, those beautiful words. I dropped the towel and went right over to the mirror and felt like the most beautiful goddess. I love a guy who can do that to you! His Facebook message said that he would be coming here in the next few weeks! This is all working out great; you see how the universe works? The last time he came with his kids, I wasn't ready to see him, wasn't in a good place, and now I am feeling great and can't wait! There is something very Michael Buble about him. I think I mentioned that before. It will be a little scary for me but I think he will know how to handle me. It's so amazing that six years ago I ran away and here I am ready and able to see him for a weekend. I have to admit that when I got his text I was really happy. I didn't sleep that well. My energy was soaring.

I am going to stay in this great place and go even deeper with it. I am determined to get to my ideal weight and to keep manifesting my soul mate. After all, who knows who it really is? There is so much to look forward to.

IT'S JUST A BIRTHDAY

I spent my birthday with my kids, we had a fun dinner at 5 Napkin Burger in the city and they got me the cutest gifts. My son sent flowers from college—God, did I cry. He's never done anything like that before on his own. What a special moment that was. I did get a text from Rhode Island. No, not a text, it was a Facebook message: "Happy Birthday! I thanked him (by text) for the birthday message and within thirty seconds I get, "hey, we need a reunion." Come on, if you want a reunion, just do it! I have already envisioned a dinner at the Delano in South Beach. Table for two, drinks on the beach, all we have to do is get rid of your "fear".

I think it's really important to add something here about "players." As you are reading this book, I'm sure you are aware there are a few mentioned. Players come in all shapes and sizes. The two that I happened to be involved with were great when I was married and unavailable. They knew how to play the game. It's safe for these guys to play with your heart and your feelings when they know nothing can come of it. They really don't take into consideration anyone's feelings but their own. Women get stuck because we think we are "that one girl" who is going to change their lives. We think the nicer we are, the more fun we are, the more they will like us. Here's the best lesson you will ever learn: stop trying, stop proving how great you are, and save it for someone who is worthy.

These guys do not change, they just move on to the next girl . . . because there always is a next girl. Be smart and learn from my book to lean back with men. Let the men do the pursuing. Once you get to know each other, you will get your chance to do for him too and have a well-balanced relationship. If you set the tone from the beginning, he will always know how to treat you. Keep your heart to yourself until you are totally ready to share it. Notice I didn't say *give it to him*. The only way love can really work is if you love yourself first; love yourself enough to know how you want to be treated. Men really want to be the one chasing. It's when that stops that they become less interested. A beautiful (Elizabeth Taylorish) older woman I met at a party once said to me, "Make sure that he loves you more than you love him . . . and never go to sleep in a fight." I think I forgot all about that until now, but now that I remember and have experienced the heartache of a player or two . . . I will never forget it again.

Anyway, back to the birthday. I spent the day getting my hair colored and going to the Peninsula Hotel for spa treatments. The hotel was so nice. It was a little depressing seeing couples having a nice, relaxing vacation, but I had my ninety-minute massage anyway. My eyes were so swollen and my face was completely wet from the tears dripping down my face. I couldn't believe it was 5:00 already. I had no plans other than seeing Jill and sleeping in her apartment. I thought I was going to die. This is it. It is just me, myself, and I. I am forty-nine today and all alone. No big celebration, no one to kiss, nothing. I wanted to go home but I didn't want the kids to know I was upset, so I went to Jill's. I got there and cried hysterically as she held me. She knows I will be fine and this is all part of my plan, but shit, it hurt. I just had to keep telling myself it was better than the alternative. That is what gets me through all of these tough times. Knowing I am here today because I chose to take a chance and let myself grow into the woman that I am. You also learn when you are going through these transformations that the pain does not last that long. Two hours from now there will be different feelings and different emotions. I can quickly go from pain and depression to joy and anticipation. I think it is so important in this process, as well as in life, to know that you do not have to stay in the darkness too long. You do need to really feel what hurts, but you learn how to move through it.

Neither one of us felt like going out. I was drained from crying so we went on JDate and Match.com to laugh. I decided to go on both sites for the fun of it. I will not flirt or wink, only respond. You really do not know where people are in their lives so you have to play for fun. I showed her hundreds of emails I have gotten—the nerve of half of these guys! We decided that except for "bluesurf" who was only thirty eight but really cute (and Ashton Kutcher is thirty-two) they were yuck! I said, "Let's look at the ones from Santa Monica. I want to live out west part time so why not flirt a little with LA guys?" Even though the girls in LA are hot, I think guys my age might be tired of the plastic girls and want someone who is real like me.

After checking out the girls on JDate, Jill said, "I am so happy for you. You are so much prettier and cooler looking than most of these girls." Thanks, Jill, but you are not my soul mate, unfortunately! Anyway, after winking and flirting I put it away and promised not to check. Just leave it in God's hands. I wake up the next day to a great email from "bluesurf." It was like four paragraphs, funny and sweet. Even though he is thirty-eight, it was great for the ego. What does he want with a forty-nine-year-old divorcee with three kids? Who knows? What did Ashton want with Demi? (I know I keep mentioning them but shit, don't we all want to be like them?) And so . . . online dating had begun.

Anyway, to bring you up to date, I sent a few flirts, a whole bunch to LA. There was one particular guy who sounded cool. He had just moved back there after ten years in New York. It was just nice for me to see there were some "normal" guys on JDate, or were there? For those of you who don't know, a flirt is like a poke on Facebook. It's just a sign that someone likes what they see.

The next day I get a manicure and meet my sister for lunch at Barney's. I get another great email from BlueSurf and my son calls and says my dog is limping! So much for the shopping spree. I run home and take my precious dog, Jack, to the vet and notice while I am in the office that his nail is black. The vet tells me, it could be cancer! I am besides myself. I leave the vet with plans to bring him in on Monday morning to have his toenail removed to see if it is cancerous and if it has spread. I know my dog and I know he is not himself. I leave the office and I am driving home, haunted by the thought of something happening to him. For anyone who knows Jack, he is the best, easiest, sweetest dog there ever was. He also keeps me company on those lonely weekend nights.

I decided instead of being bored this weekend I was going to make my wish board. I will be moving soon and want to take it with me. I am feeling content and not miserable and lonely like I was over the past weekends. My BlackBerry is flashing. Hmmm, Saturday night. Probably a stupid email from Victoria's Secret or something. It's an email from Santa Monica guy! "apologizing for not getting back to me sooner. Do you see what I mean by things happening when you are happy and content in your life and not *trying* to make them happen? That literally made my day, or weekend for that matter.

Sunday night was even better. I got a description of a new guy on JDate. As I read his profile, I began to realize that everything is going to work out. This guy's name was Michael. I know nothing about him other than what I read. It was as if someone was saying what you want is out there and you will find it. He was fifty-three and normally I would think it's too old, but his profile made me think positively and I began to like feeling "younger" than him. I really felt good. This changes the game for me. Maybe, even though my first choice is same age, and second choice younger than me, just maybe I like being the younger one—who knows? All of this brought me right back to Kathy Freston's book *(Expect a Miracle)*—do not plan or judge who, what, and where, just anticipate the feeling of being in love. This is really getting good. I have to remain balanced though and not fall in love with people I don't really know. I know now if I just take my time and keep working on being the true "Andrea," the soul mate will come.

Anyway, I am sure you are dying to know what it was about Michael. He was funny, and said at the end of this profile that his ideal date would be "Saying to each other—how is it that people like us are on JDate?" I loved it. I just loved that he was confident enough to say that. I loved that I felt the same way. I loved just knowing that connections are still out there, that this kind of guy exists.

When I finally meet "the one," we will both feel it so there won't be any games, doubts, or insecurities. We will be laughing and talking, but both will be thinking, *This is it. I am done. I have found her/him. And I am never going to let this person go.* I will shine my light for him because he shines for me. I will feel protected and safe with him and know how much he appreciated the fact that even though we both had to go through divorces to find each other, we appreciate and understand why. I know that twenty years ago it would have not worked. I was in a different place and so was he. We both adore our children and love each other. We look forward to being stepparents and grandparents. I know it hasn't happened yet because of timing, but when it's perfect, it will. So I thank you, Michael, whoever you are, for changing my life in a way and for giving me something to look forward to.

I just brought Jack home from the vet. After fighting with the ex about the bill (it's amazing how fighting about money becomes more important than the health of his dog), I will know in a few days what has to happen next. After watching him wear a collar and a cast and cry a lot, I have already decided he will not go through any torture. He will be Jack until the end and not a "sick Jack." I was lying with him on the floor tonight and Bluesurf texted. He did today as well. He remembered about Jack's surgery. He hasn't even met me yet, but it does feel good to not be the one doing the initial texting. I do not want to be the one initiating contact anymore and whoever is reading this book, take my advice. Don't be the texter, caller, or emailer. Be on the receiving end at least until you are in a relationship. I have learned the hard way. Do not get caught in one of those patterns. Make sure you keep your heart to yourself until it is really right.

The birthday wasn't so great, but the week ended well. You never know what tomorrow is going to bring. Lately I am looking forward to seeing what tomorrow brings. I am thinking positive, praying in the bathtub with my candles, listening to my meditation CDs, taking care of my body and face, and . . . getting ready!

CLEANSING WEEK
(MY BODY, HEART, AND SOUL)

I am finally cleansing and sticking to it! This isn't only about loosing weight, although it has been three days and I have lost three pounds, thank God! I must get the last seven off if it's the last thing I do. All of a sudden it got so hard but I am focused and determined. Besides, I need the body for whenever I finally have sex again. I want everything to be so right, not perfect because nothing is, just right. Whatever the "new" right is.

The cleanse is not only for weight lose, it teaches discipline and commitment. It's about sticking to something and not quitting. It cleanses your body by urinating constantly and the nighttime sea salt drink causes instant diarrhea—but it also cleanses your heart and soul. By getting rid of all the toxins in your body, you are also getting rid of toxic thoughts, feelings, and maybe even people. It's kind of like starting all over. After the cleanse, you feel refreshed and healthier and less inclined to fill your body with unhealthy foods. It makes you want to keep your thoughts and body pure.

I am still playing around with JDate, but my new philosophy is to just leave myself on and see what comes my way. I am not going to look anymore. It's depressing and I don't want to feel like I am desperate. So I am putting my energy into being exactly who and what I was meant to be, the better version of me, the one who is free to be herself. I must say I can't even believe some of the love letters I get from JDaters and Match.comers. Some men come off so strong. They also IM as soon as you get online! It's so annoying! Why is it always like that with the ones we don't want? I know the answer already and so do you—because the ones we want don't do that, which is why we want them.

I like when guys pop up to surprise me on my laptop or cell, but not all the time. Just a nice balance of attention and love to know he is thinking of me but is also busy (hopefully making a lot of money! Only kidding, not really). I want Mr. Soulmate to be financially secure enough that I don't ever have to worry. Well, change that. I want us both to be financially secure. I don't want to count on a man for money but it would be great if we are both successful in our careers so we can enjoy each other's company and do fun things when we're not working. I can't see myself ever not working again.

It's Wednesday night and I am finishing up with a client and I get an email: "I checked your schedule and cancelled both of your appointments tomorrow. Don't worry, I explained why. So go get a mani/pedi after work, I am taking you to Cabo in the morning. I got us a cabana and we have double massages at five o clock after the pool. You have been working hard and I am proud of you and I want you all to myself this weekend." That is what I want from the next man. I think I will keep the vision and manifest tonight! How amazing will it be when the right man does that? Notice I say WHEN and not IF, I get the chills just thinking about it. So getting upset about the men who are emotionally incapable is a waste of time. Sometimes they do trick you and you have to be on your toes. "Rhode Island" said next time he comes to NYC we can "go crazy" and I have no idea how much fun he is to shop with. Well, how would I know? Now we are both divorced and where is he?

"Playing" on Facebook! So be careful of the ones who promise so much so quickly. They do not mean it.

Players do not commit because there is always someone else who will give them what they want. I know a few of these guys. They could be so great. They are witty, fun, and "plugged in" but emotionally impaired. Someone or something has scared them and unless they don't do the work, like I have, to figure out why, they will remain on the road to nowhere.

It's important not to take things players do, personally. It took me years to understand that. I used to think it was me. Why did they not want to follow through? The reason is they aren't incapable of loving a woman like me. Do not ever forget those words and the next time you get hurt say them over and over. Also, ask yourself this: *Would my soul mate, the love of my life, ever treat me like this?* No. Then why spend one more minute on Mr. Maybe? Move on quickly so your real soul mate can find you.

I do not know if my man is going to pop up on my laptop one day or pop up in person, but I do know that I am more prepared than I was six months ago. I am starting to believe that God will know when it is right. I do know that I have changed in ways I never thought possible so the "soul mate" of last year will be different from this year. It's empowering and exciting to look forward to. It sure beats crying.

ROBYN

A few years before I decided to end my marriage, my very best friend from high school passed away from a brain tumor, which began as a melanoma on her neck! To go back a bit, Robyn lived four hours away on a horse farm on her parents' property. She still had family who lived near me, in our hometown, so she would call every so often and we would meet and catch up. She told me about the melanoma and her treatment, surgery, and chemo. She was reading Lance Armstrong's book and trying everything—even holistic remedies. Anyway, I get a call from her out of the blue saying that she wants to come spend the night with me and celebrate the fact that "she is in remission." So we went to an Italian restaurant, drank a bottle of wine, and decided to go sit in the parking lot and smoke cigarettes like in high school. I was a little weary of the fact that she was in remission and she wanted to smoke. She even kept saying her throat hurt but she wanted to "pretend" we were in high school. I had a funny feeling she knew something was wrong. Why else would someone in remission be smoking? I did not want to believe it, but something inside of me knew she was dying. You have to understand Robyn was a beautiful, thin, smart blonde. Her mom was a gorgeous Norwegian woman and her dad Italian. She went to Georgetown and could eat like a man and not gain a pound! She was my best friend throughout high school. We both went out with older football players and senior year had a great time being reunited with our class again. When I think about high school, it's all about Robyn and I.

We went back to my house after talking for two hours in the car. Our conversations always got very heavy and, for the first time ever, I revealed that I was not happy. Robyn was divorced twice; she had a daughter and son from different fathers who were split up when Robyn passed away. I thought that was so unfair, but legally it's what had to be done. Anyway, Robyn said to me, "Please don't continue to live like this." She made me promise. She slept over and, in the morning, typical Robyn was making herself a five-course breakfast when I woke up. Even though we didn't see each other that often, she said, "I feel so comfortable in your house. It's like the old days." And that is how it was. No matter when we spoke or saw each other, we always went right back to high school. She left that day and we said we have to do it again soon and not wait so long!

Life takes over and everyone gets busy and I was having my own personal crisis. I hardly spoke to anyone about my stuff, so after a few months I called Robyn and could not get an answer. Finally I reached her mom who told me Robyn was not doing very well and gave me her friend (relative of hers) Suzie's number. I called Suzie immediately and she filled me in. Robyn's cancer was worse. Her speech was impaired, she didn't recognize most people most of the time, and one side of her face was paralyzed from a stroke. I told Suzie I would be there the next day. The next morning Robyn's sister called and told me to wait because Robyn had a horrible night and was too weak. OMG, am I not going to say good-bye? Will I ever see her again? A few days passed and I finally got a call that Robyn was in hospice and the family decided I should come. My instincts were right all along. Robyn had not come to see me because she was in remission . . . She came to say good-bye.

I went through every photo album looking for pictures to bring so she might remember me. I took the four-hour drive myself to upstate

New York, listening to "Moondance" (Van Morrison) in her honor. When I finally got there, Suzie came outside to prepare me. Does anything prepare you for seeing one of your best friends who is dying at age forty-six? I knew I had to maintain my composure for Robyn. I walked into the room to someone who was no longer my gorgeous high school best friend. Her fun, loving spirit had gone away. She did not recognize me, she only kept asking for her daughter. Suzie said she would not know who I was, but I told Suzie I was not leaving until she did. I sat there for three hours holding her hand, showing her pictures. She would look at me from time to time but mostly fade in and out of consciousness. Finally she looked at me and says after three long hours, "Andrea, a blast from the past." The whole room began to cry. I knew it would happen. There was no way I was driving home or living the rest of my life without Robyn knowing I was there. Always listen to your gut and never, ever give up if you believe in something.

Now it was time to start my long ride home. It was beyond painful to say good-bye, not only to Robyn but to all of our high school memories. I said my good-bye and told her I loved her and I whispered into her ear, "I promise I will be happy for both of us. I promise I will not merely survive. I promise to live the next fifty years for both of us." To this day, when I am having a tough time, I look up to the sky and know she is watching me and always will be.

Robyn passed away the next week. I spoke to Suzie every day. She knew so much about our high school days. It was as if they were Robyn's greatest memories. At the funeral, her family after not seeing me for about twenty years embraced me with such love it was as if they were consoling me instead of vice versa. Her mom and I just hugged in silence for a long time. I went to Robyn's parents' house after the funeral and I noticed a house in the backyard sitting on top of a hill. I asked if that was Robyn's and her mom said, "Yes, you can go in. It's open." I took a walk up the hill and walked into a house with a ramp, wheelchair, medicine bottles, and cancer books. It was like a scene from a movie. It was the home of someone who tried desperately to live. Lance Armstrong's book was right there next to her bed. It was a cute, country house, very homey. I went up to Robyn's bedroom and sat on the bed and cried my eyes out because I wish she had called me sooner. Knowing her, she didn't want me to see her suffering. I guess she wanted our last visit to be our last.

There are no words to describe the part of me that died with Robyn. I never went to another high school reunion. I do not read "My Life" email. I do not open alumni mail. I hold my high school memories dear to my heart, but they are with Robyn now. I guess it is my way of honoring her. All of my friends this year went to their thirty-year reunions and had the best time. But for me, my reunion will always be the last night we shared together drinking a bottle of wine in my car and smoking cigarettes, just like in high school. Robyn knew that night she had come to say good-bye and that that would be our reunion . . . and it was.

WHAT A DIFFERENCE A DAY MAKES

As I sit here tonight, I honestly cannot believe what is going on in my life since I made my wish board. When you are reading the end of my book sometime soon, I guarantee you will be at the store buying Kathy Freston's book and CDs, a board, magazines, candles and calling me for coaching. I know that intuition is what guides us. It's our inner knowing that begs us to do what we need to do. It's what makes us realize we are not wrong or crazy and it is not a fantasy, it is just intuition. For so many days and nights I sat here torn between my thoughts and my life. Was I just imagining what life would be like if things were different? Something kept nagging me day in and day out to move on, to allow myself to finally grow into who I needed to be without anyone stopping me. I had to stand on my own. I could not be stopped or I would eventually just blend into the walls. I began to feel that suburbia wasn't even for me anymore. I couldn't even go out for lunch or shopping. There had to be more. And here I am writing a book about my transformation, I have a publicist, I have a website, and I am being published in a real magazine tomorrow. I am busy with real work every day. If I don't have a blog to write or any work to do, I work on my book. So for anyone reading this who doesn't know what to do with their lives and feels passionless, please know that I was there too. I was so distraught that sometimes I never thought anything would ever get me excited again. I could not be happier with my work life. I have made new friends and contacts and keep making more every day. People are joining my Facebook fan page everyday and even following me on Twitter! I took my story, a dream, and I am making it happen. By changing my life, I have organically created a career for myself.

Eventually I will be able to do all the things for myself and my kids that I dreamed about. I always tell them about the apartment in the city and one in Santa Monica I want to have and lately I think they even sense it all coming. But, regardless of what money this brings me, I found something I am passionate about, something I look forward to doing every day. Something that keeps my mind sharp and my emotions balanced. Something my intuition told me about a long time ago. Something I could never have done if I stayed in my marriage.

One night I was so discouraged looking at the New York men on JDate. I know I am generalizing, but there are so many "never been married," boring, fifty-year-olds who look seventy. Yuck . . . I thought about it and I said, "I think the kind of guy I want is not in New York. I looked at my wish board and realized there is so much LA on it so I began to check out LA men on JDate.

Well, I had a field day. Finally healthier looking, cute guys. I also wondered what guy across the country wants to get involved with someone in New York with kids, but hey, you never know, right? So I flirted with a few of them and got many responses. They read my profile so they knew I had kids and I live in New York. Why not just put it out there? You never know. Sometimes we have to just go with it.

I told you about "Jake." He's the one who emailed me while I was making my board. Anyway, this weekend I got another great email from him saying he was coming to NYC in two weeks for the premiere of his show. He will only be here for two nights, but he wants to meet! I like this; he lives in LA, writes comedy, and sends great emails. I responded I would love to meet him. He said, "If the first date goes well, when I come out in April (kids' vacation) then we can get married and both write on the beach!" I know not to take it literally, but yeah, a sense of humor! I love that. (Or it could be that "emotionally unstable" coming on too strong thing.) So many JDaters have these long profiles about love and companionship and blah blah blah. I get bored just reading them! So this will be interesting and pretty cool meeting a guy who is coming to the city for a premiere. After all, I *am* dying to get onto the red carpet!

Bluesurf popped back in this weekend also and wanted to know if "we can get together this week before someone sweeps me off my feet." I like this attention right now. (We won't go into all of the twenty-somethings and under thirty-fives who have been emailing and IM-ing me; it is kind of fun). Besides, look at Madonna, Susan Sarandon, and Demi Moore. All older and dating thirty-year-olds. I IM-ed one for about an hour the other night. This is what is missing with the fifty-year-olds: the fun and playfulness. God, I miss that. No wonder Demi is always smiling, plus these guys have stamina! I got two private callers this weekend. It makes me crazy not knowing if it's Mr. X or not. He still has a place in my heart but little by little he is getting squeezed out!

When I began writing this book, I knew somehow, someday, things would be different and better. I knew I would feel better about myself, but here's what I want all of you reading this to know: I never knew how good being *me* again could feel. I shouldn't say *being me* again because this is really a new me, this is the me I wish I knew when I was growing up. I know we can never look back, but I wish the person I am now could go back to camp, high school, and college and be secure and confident. So much of my life would have been different. So many relationships with friends and boyfriends would have been different. Most importantly, the emotions and heartache of relationships gone wrong would not have been so hard on me. If I had self-esteem back then, and a loving home environment, my life would have been probably closer to what it is now. I do not have regrets. I know the lessons had to be learned the hard way. One of my goals is to help young people avoid a lot of heartache by helping them work on their inner beauty and self-esteem issues to avoid making mistakes.

A year ago today I was unsure and afraid, and today I am cleansing and feeling great. My body is reflecting my happiness. I have a date coming up this week. I am meeting a TV writer who already wants to "marry me." Just so you all know, I put a black and white picture up on JDate. I am standing up and it's kind of a side view, nothing crazy. I am smiling, not posed, not much makeup—it just shows my true spirit. The spirit that was buried somewhere in my body for so long. The spirit that had died in a marriage gone wrong. The spirit I knew would one day emerge again. However, I had no idea it would emerge beyond my expectations. My beliefs were so limited for a while. You really have no idea what your life can become until you begin to take the steps to change it. Some days you feel great but then the next day can be even better.

I am much more prepared for the love of my life now. I waited and literally stayed home for a year and refused to go on dating sites. I took the time to really get comfortable with being alone. I got to know myself inside and out. I try to encourage single friends to do the same. When people get divorced or are suddenly alone again for whatever reason, they make a huge mistake and run out to find the next relationship or to find someone to "save" them. I am totally guilty of it myself; I didn't really do it, but I did obsess over certain people for a while. It is only when I totally let go that things began to change for me. I finally understood what Kathy Freston meant about "clearing the vessel." She meant to clear out the thoughts and emotions that keep you stuck, and when the vessel is clear, you have room for positive energy to take over. You can literally feel the energy take over; it's invigorating. I now coach my clients to spend the time getting to know who they are so they do not repeat the same old destructive relationship patterns.

I like that men find me pretty, I love reading the emails, I like that I am letting them pursue me (teaching my daughter that one)! I love that I am not trying to make anything happen anymore. The best part of the whole experience is the reason I am writing this book for you, it's not about the makeup or hair— it's because I am *happy*. I have been reading about this radiance and magnetism for four years now, but now I am living it. My self-help books are on my shelf for reference but I no longer run to Barnes and Noble every day for another one. I am writing my own. I am a woman just like you who just lost herself in an unhappy relationship. I was passionless and stagnant. I was a few days away from becoming a "Stepford Wife" and here I am today living my dreams.

Whether you are contemplating divorce or want to make your marriage better, it all comes down to how you feel about yourself. You can change your life within a relationship or choose to do it alone; it is not about the outside influences, it is all about what is happening on the inside. Life can be challenging and scary, I know I used to shake with anxiety. Do not forget only seven months ago I had a benign tumor and indigestion problems due to the stress of divorcing someone with anger issues. I am far from perfect and have learned the hard way, but I want everyone reading my story to feel the happiness I feel. So keep meditating, manifesting, and working on you. It does pay off and the rewards are indescribable. I know I will face challenges again and have good and bad days, but I also know that the bad days do not last. Life is really what you make of it, and more importantly what you *believe*.

A NEW SOUL MATE

Whoever is causing you pain, giving you false hope, not returning calls, emails, or texts, let them all go! It's not easy at first, but it begins to feel better than missing, wanting, and praying for the wrong one. Remember LA guy? The other day we were emailing about his new show that is airing next week and I emailed him my article that was just published. He sent me an email about the article, this is more like it.

I am so tired from not sleeping because Jake emails late (12:30ish EST; he's west coast) but I love reading them. I booked a trip to LA for the kids and me in April. I am staying in a hotel and the kids are staying with their aunt. If all goes well, I will be spending time with Jake. (His brother is a famous actor so I had to change names.)

The "thing" with Jake has made me realize something else. Look at him and Bluesurf, the two I chose to go out with out of all the others. Neither one of them is your standard, yuppie city slicker. Maybe the traditional kind of marriage isn't for me; maybe I need something different in my life. I always knew that the married suburban lifestyle was not enough for me. Lately I am so thankful I no longer live like that, and I am so glad I chose to spend time alone. I did everything my way and I know it will eventually work out.

How much fun will this be, having a boyfriend in LA? I love that he thinks I am sexy, it's such a turn on to me, it makes me feel even hotter, it takes me to a new level, and I want to be the sexiest I can be. Do I finally have someone who will appreciate my body that I work so hard on? It's so important to be with someone who brings out your sexiness. Don't forget that it is even more important to find it first on your own. That way no one can ever take it away from you. I love when a guy calls me sexy, especially when it's not about anything I have done in bed . . . yet! It takes a certain kind of guy, a secure one, to be able to tell you that you do something to his senses! I think it's hot.

Did I mention that I lost ten pounds on my cleanse? I manifested all of this: my long hair, my body in great shape, and a great guy! I also have so many new Facebook fans for work.

Remember my birthday? I cried through a massage and here I am with a new "playmate". This is why you have to spend the days in between the lonely ones working on your own happiness. You never know what day or what time another soul mate is going to pop in again!

I MISS THE OTHER JAKE

I am sure you can tell by the title that in real life Jake was nothing like "cyberspace Jake." Wow, did I have that all wrong. At least I got a better feel for what I want through all of this.

Let me start by telling you we had a huge hurricane last Saturday. Today is Wednesday and we are still without power. Jack (my dog) who is not well had to stay with my ex. My daughter stayed at my mom's with me. It wasn't easy being in that house with all of the pictures of my dad and mom in the married years. Anyway, I made the best of it as always. Jake had been emailing that he was watching the hurricane on the Internet and he was being really supportive.

Finally Jake landed in New York and called me BUT, this wasn't the Jake I have been emailing. It just didn't sound like who I had pictured. I told myself to give it a chance and realized maybe he was nervous. I think I knew right then and there . . . this wasn't the right "Jake." He was coming for the premiere of his own show for Comedy Central and was staying at some Comfort Inn in Chelsea? What? I guess dinner at Nobu with my writer wasn't happening!

When you do not have a real conversation with someone, and you are relying on emails and texting, your imagination can really get carried away! He was definitely pleasant looking, but not who I thought he would be. Much more hyper and a lot of ex-wife talk! He isn't divorced yet and was at that stage where you are "done" but still trying to figure it out. Plus the daughter lives here and he's in LA. We did have a nice talk. I think I told him a little too much, but he was easy to talk to. This was one of my first dates and I did really well. I held my own; I ignored his constant reminder about how I could stay in his hotel with him. Men! I was confident and fun, and it was great practice. It was just so weird how I pictured his essence and how different he was in real life. Big lesson here: a few days of emails are okay, but then you must speak on the phone. You can still text and email, but there has to be some real contact. A person's voice says so much about them. I never realized how much until now. I was definitely bummed but I realized the guy who I wanted him to be is still out there . . . that is what it means. No reason to eat a pint of Ben and Jerry's. It's just going to take more time.

I wrote on my fan page today: "If a person turns out to be not what you expected, don't worry because the right one is still out there looking for you!" The new me does believe this is true.

I learned more about my real soulmate by meeting this one. I felt what the real one will feel like. I liked the consistency we had. I waited to hear from him and did, and I also emailed him when I wanted to. I was serious and flirty and so was he. So we learn from every relationship even if they are just in cyber space.

By the way, Great One emailed today to have fun on my date and we emailed when I got home. So nice to have my cyber buddy. He is always there for me. He will have to remain a cyber buddy, although he keeps asking me out. He is twenty-eight —so not happening! I think thirties would be okay though. You know I love the Demi and Ashton thing, but twenty-eight is a little young. He is mature and fun though.

Maybe . . . bluesurf? Who knows? Where is Mr. X? How could he ever really never speak to me again? He will never find better! I know we all say that when are angry, but I really mean it!

So the saga continues. I need a JDate break, it's really not my thing.

SETBACKS

It's funny. Last week I was thinking about how I was going to have a long-distance relationship with someone in LA and today I am back to a "not so great place." If I had not done all of the self-work, I would be borderline suicidal right now! My house deal fell through. I have a flood to take care of with an ex who doesn't exactly "fix things" the right way or care if his children are living in a house with black mold! (It's always about the money with him, even over health!) The worst part is . . . Jack's (my dog) cancer diagnosis was confirmed and he will have to be put to sleep soon. My other options are amputation and chemo. I stayed home with him all weekend and cried! "Great One" was emailing me all weekend on his BlackBerry. He makes me laugh and he's sweet. He even emailed from a bar mitzvah last night how the kids' food was so much better than the grownups'! Shit, why is he so young! He is another soul mate though; he is showing me what I need in a guy. He's deep at times, but has a great sense of humor. And I know this is hard to believe, but he knows women better than a lot of forty-nine-year-olds I know. Other than that, it was a lonely weekend.

I have to admit I am really scared of losing Jack. At least on Saturday nights I know he is always home with me. You really do not realize how much you love your dog until something like this happens. I wrote a letter to Dr. DeMichael, the breeder who I got Jack from. I told him about Jack's diagnosis and thanked him for breeding such an amazing dog. I never thought I would consider getting another dog after Jack, but lately I am thinking about the next one. I think even though I was never a "dog person," once you have one, you always want one. My dog is the one guy right now that loves me "unconditionally." He comes to me every few minutes to let me know he is in pain. He doesn't cry. We both just understand he will have to go soon.

My house deal is falling through. The people lowered their price and I am not taking it. I can't believe I just can't seem to move on (physically). I want a new place with new sheets, towels and energy. I have been so patient. I still have to believe that all of this is happening for a reason and that things are going to turn around for me. My business is what keeps me smiling these days. I have one hundred fans on Facebook and they are starting to respond to my quotes! I always respond back. I love the communication. I always loved helping people. I still have my purpose and that is what counts.

As far as my love life goes, I am back to square one. Nothing lost, only gained. Even though Jake turned out to be the wrong one, I learned more about "the one" through him. This is the purpose for relationships; they are all lessons of some sort. It's funny. I was crying my eyes out Saturday when the vet called me. I was in town with my son and we went into CVS to get toothpaste (life goes on!). I bumped into an old friend, and I told her about Jack, whom she knows well. We hugged and cried and an old soul mate walked by with his kids. I was crying and he was so sweet and asked if everything was okay and I told him it was my dog. He gave me those sweet puppy eyes and asked if everything else was okay. I said yes. I hadn't even thought about him in such a long time. I always respected him for having gone through a major life transformation. Anyway, that night I was hanging with Jack and playing on Facebook and sent him a message to join my fan page.

The next day he friended me. The past seems to come back. It's nice to have him on my Facebook if not for any other reason . . . he's good to look at. Where is my real soulmate? Like Oletta Adams says in her song, "I don't care how you get here . . . just *get here!*"

IT IS ABOUT THE JOURNEY,
NOT THE DESTINATION

It seems like I started this book three years ago! I can't believe it has only been about eight months. So much has changed and so much has happened. There have been hard days for me, but some pretty great ones too. I have to be honest and say the great ones definitely outnumber the crappy ones! Sometimes I have to just stop and remember that I left an unhappy situation. It took every bit of strength that I had. I would never go into too much detail out of respect for my children. I will say no one will ever bring me down or put me down again. I will never have toxic people in my life again. I have some pretty great new friends who are healthy and positive.

Even though Great One is thirty years old we have gotten to be pretty good friends. He is texting me right now from the Seder table. It is passover and I asked him if he was reading the four questions, LOL! (The four questions are read by the youngest person at the table, usually a child). I might not be with the "one" yet, but I have some fun new people in my life this year. I am not really attracted to the typical yuppie suburban dad, at least not that I have met yet. The emails winks and flirts from JDate and Match.com are getting worse and worse. I still believe I am going to meet my man in person; it has always been my MO. I had no problem meeting guys pre-JDate. I think it's so much easier to meet organically (I love that word) in person because you already know what each other looks like.

I really do not like dating. I just want to meet someone and hang out and see where it goes. I am sure my soul mate is feeling exactly the same way. I think we do the online dating game because that is what society tells us to do, but deep down most of us hate it. There are a lot of success stories I know but I hear just as many horror stories. Just from my own experience, I know people either aren't what I perceive them to be or they lie about their age, put old or even other people's pictures on their profiles, or they aren't really divorced—or even separated for that matter. Have they not heard of www.ashleymadison.com? So be careful not to reveal too much about yourself too soon. You don't really know who anyone is.

I think I am doing well considering my dog is dying of cancer, my parents are divorcing, my house is still not sold, and my ex continues to be abusive and difficult. I have just had to deal with a lot at one time. Thank God my for future business and for this book! I was interviewed by *Glamour* magazine last week about "relationship issues," "man baggage," etc. A writer told me on the spot that I will be in their July issue! This is really big; we know how many women read *Glamour*! Even more importantly, I am speaking from experience and I speak from the heart. I am so passionate about my journey and how it can help others that it just comes naturally for me to talk about.

One of my best friends texted me yesterday knowing I was sad about not having my own "new family" for the holidays. She said, "You are honest and truthful and my heart breaks understanding how you feel. You have done everything with such grace and class and continue to do so . . ." recognizing my courage and strength like that is *priceless* to me . . . Thanks, Heller.

It was very difficult detaching from my ex. I am now free to live on my own terms. My closest friends and family understand even if he can't or won't. I let so much go, but I do have my moments when I start getting anxiety from the contact. I know I have to acknowledge the feelings and let them go so they can pass. For those of you reading this who may be in a similar situation, the anxiety and fear do lessen as each day passes. As you begin to meet positive, kind, loving people who also make you laugh, you realize there are some really good people out there. I think when you are in the wrong situation for a long time you forget what kindness and humanity are like. I am here to tell you I feel more loved than I ever have before. Yes, many friendships that I used to have no longer exist, but the ones who are here with me today, I cherish. I have some friends now that I can just call and cry to and the same people get the "happy" calls too. Real friends are the ones who feel your pain. Because of them, I have become a better friend. I have just become a better person all around because I am free and able to have my own thoughts and my own life.

As you might guess, I am still a hopeless romantic! The difference is I am not afraid to dream; I am no longer questioning fantasy from reality. I do believe in a certain kind of love. The experiences I am having are showing me to stay on course. Even though my soul mate is still working on himself and isn't ready to appear, I get glimpses of him from the other guys I have met. I know that I don't like the games. I know I can express what makes me happy without being afraid I will scare them away. I know a sense of humor is very important, even in emails and texting. I know I have to be able to be funny and they have to "get me." I also know what it's like to get emails and texts that aren't only two words long. I am just beginning this part of my journey. Eventually I will be speaking to and touching the special guy who makes my heart beat. Therefore, I believe God will take care of me and I am learning slowly about myself and what I need in a soul mate.

Coming from an unaffectionate home environment as a child has definitely affected me, but I have learned to use it as a lesson as opposed to dwelling too much in the pain of it all. Yes, most of us wish we could go back and redo our childhoods, but if so, we would not be the people we are today. I look at my own marriage as a lesson as well. Although it has only been a year since I am divorced, it has been one of a lot of reflection and soul searching. My divorce has led me to immeasurable amounts of growth, which could have never happened had I stayed in my situation. Growth is painful, hence, the phrase, "growing pains." The good days outweigh the bad and the good gets better and better. I still dream about the day I can look into my soul mate's eyes and know exactly why my journey happened the way it did. I know who that person looking into his eyes will be; the me I always dreamed I could be.

JACK

Here's the thing about this book, or life I should say: whoever thought in a billion years I would be writing a chapter about losing my dog to cancer? Today is the day we are putting Jack to sleep. What started as a lump turned out to be bone cancer. We had many ups and downs that began with the removal of his toenail. The reports turned out to be inconclusive, which led to a bone biopsy. The last two months I did everything I could: increased medication, decreased medication, and finally when I came home from LA I felt like Jack was telling me he was really hurting. I knew he waited for me to get home to make the decisions and be by his side. I always had the option of putting him to sleep but knew I would fight till the end, as always. I finally made the decision with the vet to try a pain patch. Jack was no longer eating, nor would he take any more pills (the first sign that he wanted *out)*. Just to let you know how special he is, every time I walked into the vet's office in the last two months, everyone including the office staff would get teary. One day I even said to them, "Come on, you guys deal with this every day." They said, "Jack is different. He is such a great dog and he has never been sick except for ear infections and you are so nice." I asked them at that point what I should do and they said he is not Jack anymore, let him go. I decided at that point to try the three-day pain patch. I needed to know I did everything in my power, but unfortunately he continued deteriorating.

I woke up Monday, April 12, and made the call. I dialed and when they picked up all I had to say, or all I could say, was, "It's Andrea Gross." I was too hysterical to speak. I just said, "Saturday." This week has been an intense buildup for my kids and I haven't stopped crying from all the stress. I got so sick, I have a sinus infection. I went to the doctor yesterday to get antibiotics because I need my strength to get my kids through this.

Today I went to pick up a pill hoping Jack would take it for pain. My two favorite office girls started hugging me and telling me they wouldn't be there Saturday, it was their day off. That was not happening so I changed "the big day" to Friday. I want them with me. It's funny, throughout life we meet employees at different places, especially at our regular stops, and if you are kind to them and show your respect you end up developing an unconditional relationship, which at times like this ends up being your support system. A true lesson to always treat people well.

So here I am at my computer and Jack is on the couch in front of me. He has been hanging there while I write this book for the last couple of months. Today is the last day he will sit and watch me work on my book. I know he will always be here in spirit. I have decided to have him cremated so he is always with me. I would do anything for him to get up right now and get mud on my bed or shed all over my brown leather couch, and beg for fresh turkey from the deli— do all of the things that use to drive me crazy. I just want the old Jack back for one more day, but that isn't the way it works. I have to admit I am a little scared of being without him. In one year I get divorced, my oldest son goes to college, and I am losing my dog. I think that's a lot for one single mom to handle, don't you?

Jack is the one who is always home when I am here by myself at night and I live in a big house. Although he is the worst watchdog. (no matter who walks in my door, he lies at their feet to be rubbed!) He watches all of my chick flicks with me and watches me cry. He has been through everything with me and knows when to lick my face and when to leave me alone. It's amazing how close you can be with a living creature that can't even speak! Last night I put a picture of Jack on my wish board. My daughter said to put him on there so he will bring good things to me. My best friends have their standard things to say, the same thing they said when I had my fibroid tumor removed, when I got divorced, when my parents split, and when I told them about today. One said, "Hang in there . . . you will be fine. You always are." Another said, "After this, all good things." And last but not least, "Your house is going to sell and in will walk that amazing soul mate you have been praying for. You deserve something so wonderful and have handled everything with dignity and grace." That is what gets me through the day. Plus, my daughter telling me Jack would make sure good things happen to me.

I feel bad my oldest son is away at college. I gave him the option to fly home, but he is far away in Arizona. I know his heart is with us, I just wish he was here for his sister and brother. It's hard being divorced and having no relationship with your ex at times like this. I feel like my other son who is now the oldest child at home has a lot of weight on his shoulders, being the man of the house. Last night my daughter slept with me and began to cry saying, "No one will ever be like Jack." I told her no one will ever be like Jack, but one day another dog will be just as great. Not better and not worse, just different. I explained to her it's the same with people. People come in and out of our lives at different times for different reasons. Sometimes they stay forever and sometimes they don't. In time we learn why and every relationship is meant to teach us things, whether good or bad. I told her we need to not be selfish today, we need to think about what is best for Jack.

I texted RI yesterday just to let him know about Jack. I know deep down he has a good heart. He texted right back that it must be difficult and he hopes I am okay. Last week I watched the movie *Serendipity*, the one with Kate Beckinsale (love her) and John Cusack about a guy and a girl who meet in Bloomingdale's and have a great day together even though they both have significant others. She won't give him her number because she says, "If it's meant to be, we will be together someday." I don't want to ruin the movie for you, but they do end up together after several years. They come together at a time that is right for both of them and when they do, it's magical! Don't forget they hardly knew each other; it was really only one day they shared together. So of course the hopeless romantic in me wonders about some of my own soul mates still lurking in the back of my mind. Maybe I will have my very own *Serendipity* . . .

MY LIFE IS A STEVE CARRELL MOVIE

You would not believe what happened to me yesterday. I picked my kids up early from school so we could spend some time with Jack before his 3:00 "being put to sleep" appointment. The minutes were as long as hours as we waited in anticipation. I just wanted it to be over, but at the same time I didn't want it to happen at all. It was also going to be the first time I would be in the same room as my ex since the "grand finale" at court, but it was his dog too. It was finally almost three o'clock and we began getting ready to leave. My son was taking his own car and would follow me. I told my housekeeper when I left to take every bit of food, bones, toys, his bed, every reminder of Jack and give it all to her sister who had a dog and to please have it all gone before I got home! I want the only memories to be the ones in my heart. Seeing Jack's toys in the house would destroy me.

I took Jack to the backyard for his last pee. At this point I am hysterical I can hardly breathe. This was it. It was real. It took my son, my daughter, and me to get Jack into the car. He was so weak. He had lost weight but was still ninety pounds. We were heading down a major hill and I noticed there was a landscape truck behind me so I go to pull over to let him pass but the idiot isn't watching and sideswipes my car so badly

I thought Jack was a goner. I thought for a brief second maybe God wanted him to go this way. No, it couldn't be. I turned around to look and Jack, he was safe and sound. I was screaming crying at his point. It was now three o'clock and the nurses I wanted with me (the reason I switched the appointment to today) would be leaving at four o'clock. Luckily an undercover cop was passing by and pulled over. OMG, to top it off it was my ex's secretary's husband! I begged him to help me because I had about two minutes to get to the vet. I asked him to leave my car on the street. It was not drivable and I would deal with it later. My son managed to coast it down the hill and get it on to a side street. We got my dog out and into my son's car and drove to the vets office, we were all in shock, crying and scared.

When we arrived at the office, my favorite nurse came out to the car and hugged me. My ex carried Jack in and all of a sudden, there we were in a room waiting to put Jack to sleep. It took longer than expected to put Jack down because his circulation was so bad from the cancer, he needed an extra shot. As soon as he got the first shot which tranquilized him, I was at peace. I knew then that maybe I waited a little longer than I should have. I knew he was finally out of pain. I held his paw the whole time and stroked his face. I told him I was sorry if I waited too long for this but I loved him and didn't want to let go. As he left this world, I knew he would be watching over me forever. I told my kids he was now with his parents somewhere in doggie heaven eating fresh turkey (his favorite). My daughter said he would now be my guardian angel. (Thank God. The more the merrier!) The whole thing took about half an hour. I don't think I have any more tears left in me. I have never cried like that before in my entire life.

We were finally ready to leave and my ex says, "Just call triple A's to tow your car." I tell him, "I can't, you canceled mine." (That's divorce talk)! My son takes me to my car and I call the insurance company, tow truck, etc . . . and while we are there one of my neighbors, a true character, drives by in her Mercedese and says, "OMG, what happened to you guys?" It's like a comedy because my ex is there in his car and

I am there in mine and I said to her, "Forget the car. I just put Jack to sleep." I am still shaky and crying and she says, "Well, you look great!" How's that for suburbia? She says, "Do you need anything?" I said, "Just a Valium." (I have never really taken one.) She says in perfect suburbia lingo, "Just come over. I have whatever you need!"

Anyway, I finally got home, had the car towed, and lied down on my Jackless bed. It was brutally quiet in the house without Jack, but luckily the kids went out and weren't home to think about it. I think deep down, although we miss him terribly, we are relieved not to be watching him suffer anymore. I got into my bed and watched TV and got a new Facebook message from an old soul mate I had recently reconnected with. We had both been in tough places in our marriages at the same time; he got divorced a few years before me and now had this whole new life. It was so great to cyber speak with him. We spoke more than we ever did back then. It's nice when old friends come back.

I called my three BFFs to tell them about what happened. We laughed, we cried. The things that happen to me cannot be made up. I swear. I bumped into one of my BFF's husbands at CVS tonight while I was buying "feeling sorry for myself candy". He knew about yesterday with the accident and Jack and he said to me, "You are a Steve Carrell movie. You couldn't make this stuff up . . . Keep going girl."

YOU'RE NOT REALLY DIVORCED UNTIL YOU PACK UP YOUR HOUSE!

The packing fun has just begun! Let me start by telling you it's Memorial Day weekend 2010. My kids are in the Hamptons with their dad, who hated the Hamptons when we were married. He didn't want to deal with traffic and only wanted to buy a house at the Jersey Shore, okay? But who cares? I hope they all have fun. To let you know how far I have come, yesterday I went into the city early after a long run and saw *Sex and the City 2* by myself. I walked around the city for a little while and went to a few stores to start looking at furniture and things for our new place, the one I haven't found, but the one I know is going to work out just fine. The movie was fun, funny, and everything I thought it would be! After the movie, I went to Aimee for my facial acupuncture (love) and then met with a client at 7:30. As I drove home at 9:00 p.m., thinking I was the only person on earth with no plans this weekend, the tears began to fall. I was going home to my empty house—my girl toys await! I want it to be so right and if it takes a while to meet that lucky guy so be it! Back to the tears. As the tears began to come down, I stopped myself quickly and thought, *Holy shit! All I wanted was to have my own coaching business* (check), *write my book* (check), *move to a new house that is all me, with new energy where I can manifest my soul mate in my own space* (check, almost), and my tears of sadness quickly became tears of joy! I am really living my dream. It is slowly unfolding.

The next day I woke early and went for a run, bought some boxes, got a green tea at Starbucks and went to work packing! I even put the stereo on. Cinderella is whistling a happy tune while she works! Do you know that for the last twelve years I have lived in this house I have never put the stereo on in the living room? I had to figure out how to do it today. That's how happy I am—or how unhappy I was. Yes, I get sentimental packing the pictures and the DVDs of happy memories, but that's okay. I am human. It's hard to decide what to throw away and what to keep. I am keeping most of it for my kids. Yes, it is a fact that their father and I were married for twenty years and the moments captured in the pictures really happened and were happy ones. Why shouldn't they have memories of that? After all, we will be Grandma and Grandpa someday and we do have a history. So many people have trouble talking about their past, but that's not realistic. That is denial. I am trying to talk about it more with my kids to let them know that at one time, their parents did love each other and did create them out of love. I can't blame them for not understanding because sometimes it is hard for me to even remember those feelings. Sometimes my kids will tell me something they remember and sometimes it was bad and sometimes it was good. Kids are smarter than we give them credit for.

Last night I was reading a book about wedding vows. Traditionally we promise to stay together in sickness and health, but I think when we say our vows we are referring to sickness as physical sickness. We don't think about someone's past creeping up on them and affecting how they treat the people they love. We also don't think at the time, *What if one of us grows and evolves and the other one stays where they are? Is the one who is trying to grow supposed to sacrifice her life to stay stagnant and unhappy? What if one of us needs to grow and the other won't allow it?* I think if we thought about these things, none of us would ever get married! What twenty-something is thinking about these things when all they want to do is get married and have children? The book I am reading, *The Vortex,* suggested these kinds of vows: "It is my dominant intent to focus my thoughts in a positive direction so that I maintain my connection with the Source and the love that is really who I am . . . and in doing so, I will always represent myself to you. It is my desire that you ask the same of yourself. And it is my expectation that both of us works to maintain our individual alignment with who we really are, our relationship with one another will be one of continual and joyful expansion."

Well, that takes a load off, doesn't it? Especially for us divorcees who might be a little hesitant to take that walk down the aisle again! If we both promise to be our best selves for each other and to stay focused in a positive direction, then we will have a great marriage! Wow, where was this book twenty years ago? I don't think I would have even understood what it meant back then. I will definitely make sure my children and clients understand it. We should all make a promise to our spouses to be our best selves and let them be their best selves. We want our spouse to always shine their heart lights and we have to promise not to blow it out!

SOMETIMES PLAN B
TURNS OUT TO BE PLAN A

Sometimes you wake up in the morning after a really stressful, scary day and realize, *OMG, I think I am back to plan A*. Sometimes when we want something so badly we try to force it to happen. This is true with relationships and jobs and everything in between. However, if you let time pass and work on yourself and forget about trying to make something happen, it just comes back naturally, *if* it's meant to be.

Here's what happened. I sold my house and the closing is literally in two weeks and I don't have any idea where my three children and I are going to live. Not too stressful! There was a place I found over a year ago that I loved and wanted to move into after selling my house, but deals fell through, storms came, floods came, more deals fell through, things were not fixed properly from the flood (trees are still down on my front lawn three months later because of an insurance/divorce money disagreement—another perk of being divorced and still living in the marital home LOL). Anyway, the last time I went to see the house I loved I realized it was too expensive. When I first saw it I thought my house would sell for a lot more money than it did! Even though selling it means moving on and even that is priceless, it is enough with the MasterCard commercial—this is real life! I decided I need to find a rental.

Then a miracle happened. My broker found out that someone was renting a townhouse in the same complex exactly like the one I wanted to buy and they were moving out the same week as my closing. Wow, I can rent and keep my money in the bank with no pressure to buy! Not that easy, for the last month the brokers have been trying to contact the owners to make sure I can rent and no one can find them. Every day I have been praying that we hear from them.

Yesterday was a killer day. After taking my new favorite spin class in NYC I was driving home and passed Mr. X on a road near my house! OMG, he's still alive. Thank you, God, for that sign, although I do not think about him as much as I did because I'm busy working and taking care of my kids. Anyway, about an hour after that my broker called and said, "We need a plan B just in case." My stomach dropped. My heart began to race as she told me what was available. I couldn't breathe. It's not that I am such a snob that I have to live in a fancy place, but I promised my kids we would move into the townhouse that they want and here I am disappointing them. They are getting through a divorce, we lost our dog, there is no way I am letting them down!

The day continued. I picked up my car after seven weeks of being in the body shop from the accident I had with my dog—remember? I'm finally so happy to see my car and drive out of the station. Shit, the radio has no volume, the air bag is beeping, and the RPMs are spinning out of control! I had to take it to another service place and rent a car again. So more fighting with my insurance company about the bill and I'm sure my ex will not be paying even though car repairs are his responsibility. I go and rent another car and cry the whole way home. What am I going to do about moving? I call my BFF's and they are all saying what they always say: whatever is meant to be will be; you will be fine.

I get home and I am hot and tired and depressed so I start to pack up the kitchen to distract myself and I begin to smile again. I just feel like one day I will be in my house and the doorbell is going to ring and it will be him!

I go to sleep early that night and wake up at 6:00 a.m. thinking, *OMG! I am supposed to buy the first townhouse. That is why this isn't working with the other one. My plan B is plan A.* I let it go a while ago and opened myself up to something new. I was patient and it came back in a new light. I am not nervous about it anymore. Now I know it is the right thing to do. And the same thing with Mr. X. I have not tried to contact him. I have gone on with my life. I am happy now, and patient. I am still on JDate and Match.com, and dating. Yes, I am being open but so far they are not for me. Maybe it's because I belong with Mr. X and at the right time, with me staying to myself and keeping my heart safe, when we are both ready, he will come to my plan A new home and we can have our plan A, B, C, D life together.

STEPPING AWAY MEANS
STEPPING FORWARD

I have to say that my dreams are really coming true in some ways, which leads me to believe that they will on all levels. I love working! I not only love helping people, but I love the fact that my clients look up to me and want to hear all about my story and how I got here. I had this dream that I would be a life coach and here I am in business. I did this all on my own. I told myself and my dad that I would give myself until the end of the summer and if I wasn't making money I would do something else (I knew that wasn't happening, there is nothing I would rather do), and here I am working and it is not even Memorial Day weekend yet!

I call this chapter "Stepping back means Stepping Forward" because as far as love goes, I am choosing a different path. I am neither out looking nor really paying much attention to online dating. I just "know" with patience and by continuing on this path . . . it will happen. I don't mean the knight in white shining armor; mine will be in jeans and a white shirt! I mean, if I continue to grow in the direction that I am, then the right guy will come along. I have to continue growing and changing and at the right stage of my growth, he will appear. I do not want to stop my growth ever again for a man. I want a man who compliments my growth and encourages me to reach new levels because he also is doing the same (awesome stuff!) Saturday night chick flicks and takeout can only get you so far, but it will make me appreciate my weekends even more someday. When this all turns out the way I dream it will, I am going to have such an amazing story to tell my grandchildren.

I continue to manifest every night. I used to think I knew who "the one" was or who I wanted him to be, but that is changing. I don't want to be with anyone who doesn't call me back or call to see how I am doing when my dog dies! I want a real man, one who is not afraid to show his feelings, one with class, one who likes to work but likes his play time even better. I want a real man who inspires me to be a really sexy, confident woman. I want a guy who looks at me and just "wants it!" A romantic guy who wants me all to himself and loves to show me places and things and loves to go away and stay in great hotels. Don't get me wrong: it is not about the money. If it was, I would have stayed married and would still live in my house with the pool and still have my black Porsche. It is so not about that. I just want to learn things from the next guy and not be the teacher. Yes, I do think it is important to share your knowledge and wisdom with your mate, but I want to learn as much from him as he learns from me. I want surprises; I can't do the boring routine. I want my guy to have an imagination and throw me off guard here and there. I mean really shake things up—and I definitely don't mean by being emotionally unstable, at the first sign of that I will say adios. If you are scared, commitment phobic, or bipolar, stay away from me, I beg you!

I have been there too many times. Please do not tell me you want to marry me until you really know me. Do not wait to return a call or text for two days. Do not play games with me. I am not interested and I am saving my romantic love for the right guy, and until then my energy is for me and my kids and my work. This is not a threat, I am just saying I am so ready to love again but I want it to be right. This is *my* fairytale, remember?

I decided that I am not waking up until my dream is over. I will go on with my life until the whole picture unfolds exactly how I want it to. I will continue to pray and manifest and not give up on my soul mate or myself. I know that if I begin to slip in the faith department that I have the tools to get back on track. I also know that if I slip back I will not end up with the right person. I need to continue to grow and see what the universe has in store for me.

STILL CONVINCED TO
JUST LET IT HAPPEN

Let me tell you about this past weekend. Let's start with the fact that RI was maybe going to come to NYC this weekend, *if* he didn't stay in Chicago, and I was actually thinking maybe I would see him. I even put my black cashmere halter in my suitcase to go to Patty's for the weekend, thinking I might drive into the city Saturday to see him if he called. Remember the last time he came to NYC I never went to meet him because he asked me Friday night last minute ! I was checking my cell phone all weekend thinking he might be man enough to even let me know one way or another but . . . never heard. I was disappointed in myself for even considering meeting him after he let me know I would be a second choice. Maybe he's married.

I went to Patty's for the weekend. It was so nice to get away. We had so much fun. I have to mention here my appreciation for my oldest camp friend, Patty. Patty and her husband have welcomed me into their home many times. Sometimes I pack my bag and just go there for the weekend. I cannot express enough how much their kindness and understanding means to me. When you are single and alone, the weekends can be really hard. Knowing they are always there has gotten me through some tough nights. I know one day my husband and I will be very close to them, and I know they can't wait!

Friday night we decided to go to a new "hot spot" for dinner. We had drinks first and we were feeling good and we get to the place and head straight for the bar. I take a couple of looks around and I know right away when I am going to like a place by the type of people. Anyway, we had a great laugh, I said to Patty, "these guys are the ones I rejected on JDate!" I said, "Let's get out of here!" It was so true. They were just old, Jappy men—*yuck!* I was feeling good and said to Patty, "Shit, where are the cool guys?" We ended up going to another place. I sat at the bar, and the bartender said, "How are you tonight?" I said, "So happy to be here!" I know for a lot of single people that bar scene is how they socialize, but not for me! Besides, I never see "my type" of guys hanging out in places like that. Where are they? I do not know, but certainly not there! This only confirms to me what I have been feeling all along: don't look, it will happen. The type of guy I want to meet would never be in a place like that. He is wondering where I am and will figure out how to meet me!

When I came home and went to sleep Sunday, I decided to just keep doing what I am doing and just get to a happy place every day on my own and someone will just pop into my life one day. No more texting or reaching out to guys like RI who are not smart enough to know what he is passing up! That is not coming from an angry place, it is just the truth!

I think my house is about to sell—for real this time! It's a little less money than I wanted, but at this point I just want to move and buy new things and get away from the "energy" in this house. I almost cried when they told me we were making a deal. It's very bittersweet. It is another "moving on" stage that I have to do alone. I have to handle the finances, the packing, and the feelings about moving all on my own and be strong enough for my kids who are probably having the same feelings as me. My kids have been anxious to move, I guess they want to start over as well.

Maybe I will move into my new place and Mr. Right will pop into my life. I always said that I wanted to get my business going and move and then meet "the one." Maybe that is really the plan for me. Maybe I really don't have to deal with the whole dating scene. Maybe it really will happen the way I manifest it will. Who knows? All I know is I am doing really well on my own and standing on my own two feet especially when it comes to dealing with my ex! I have gotten a lot tougher with him and continue to work on emotionally detaching..

It's hard sometimes when people say they are so happy for me because some days you feel like saying to them, "This isn't how I wanted my life to end up. I wanted to grow old with the father of my children and be grandparents together and retire and travel and finally have some fun, but that isn't how it turned out for me." I do know that I will get to do those things with someone who will appreciate my humor and love me for who I am and take care of me when I am sick or even when I am just hurting. I also know that all of that is what I really want and not just the Hallmark fiftieth wedding anniversary card. That is just about a number. I am glad to know that I will not be at my 50th anniversary dinner wondering why I am still there. It will be an amazing celebration! I will also be 100 years old!

NEW HOME . . . NEW LIFE

I am sitting in my new kitchen and it is Sunday night. I cannot even begin to explain how exciting and new everything feels. Last week I was on an emotional roller coaster. Closing on the house was a nightmare up until the bitter end. I won on the big issue of my ex paying for camp. It was already settled four months ago in court but he still tried changing it. Amazing he caved on that but stuck to his guns about me paying the seven-hundred-dollar iTunes bill that was on his credit card for this year.! He almost did not close on the house because of iTunes! The closing was scheduled to take place at 12:30, by this time I was physically and emotionally drained. It was 12:20 and I was crying in my old laundry room. The buyers had tears in their eyes just from listening to me talk on the phone trying to get the deal done. They were nice young people with two small kids and one on the way and they felt so bad for me. I finally get up the strength to call my lawyer, and say, "I will pay the f— iTunes bill. *Close!*" (This is what happens when you have to deal with a man who knows how to push your buttons after being married to you for twenty years!) At that moment I wanted to scream of happiness, "I am done forever! I will never have to go through any financial abuse from this man or any other for that matter! Take your iTunes bill, which is your kids' anyway, you fool, and shove it up your a--! How dare you treat me, the mother of your children that way!" A little post divorce venting!

To go back a bit, last week started with a tag sale. I was a little nervous at first watching all of my things get tagged. I was even scared I was going to sell some things that I should be saving, but as the three-day sale transpired, I got into it. I finally got to the point where I wanted everything out. I decided I want to buy everything new. I did it all on my own, I packed my huge house into boxes. The movers came and began moving my things out and the kids waited at the new house for furniture deliveries. I continued to do laundry and supervised, making sure the people cleaning and dumping were taking the right stuff. I did not stop working until 11:00 Friday night. I wanted everything finished. I did a great job. Cablevision came, air conditioning was working, deliveries were perfectly timed . . . I ended up signing the papers my attorney brought to my new house at 9:00 p.m. Friday night.

I have been in the new house for a week now and I cannot even describe how happy I am. I am picking everything out myself and having a blast making this a great home for my kids and me. Everything is new and fresh and mine! I knew things would be different when I moved out of the old house and away from the old energy, but I had no idea it would be this great. I know throughout this book, along the way, there have been setbacks and days of joy, but never in a million years did I think I would ever feel this free and happy. I am getting to know the real me again.

MY OWN CLOSETS

It has been a whirlwind since I moved. Every day is filled with trips to Target; Bed, Bath and Beyond; furniture stores; changing insurance policies; and at the same time "single mothering" two teenage boys and their friends and a twelve-year-old tween girl who all of a sudden thinks she is twenty-one! I must say through it all, I am damn happy. The euphoric feeling of going to stores and picking out what I like without having to consult anyone about my choices or how to pay for it is . . . priceless. I feel like I just graduated from college and I am setting up my first apartment. I have both walk-in closets filled in my bedroom—one for winter clothes and one for summer. One of my best friends came over the other day and took one look at my closets and said, "You are never going to get married again." We laughed so hard because of all I have been though this year. It is so great when you can finally laugh about it! Anyway, my response to her was, "Only if he has his own closet!" We laughed again but what I really meant by that was, *only if he has his own life.* I know what it feels like to be really happy on your own and I will only be with a guy who, like me, is happy on his own and not depending on me for his happiness and . . . comes with his own closet.

I feel like I have come full circle. I no longer have any expectations or plans and I am not hooked on outcomes anymore. This way of living is very freeing to me. When we aren't worried about the future, we can allow things to happen naturally. This way of living eliminates the fear, anxiety, and worrying. I wake up in my new bed now with a huge smile on my face and welcome the day expecting miracles, not obsessing on what hasn't happened yet.

A TRUE BLUE INDEPENDENCE
DAY FOR ME

I posted today on Facebook that last July Forth I was recovering from surgery—remember that, my ovarian fibroid tumor that turned out to be benign? That was only a year ago and today I am in my new home, totally free. No more lawyer stuff for me . . . ever! I am also completely healthy! So what if my soul mate isn't ready yet. The main thing is that I am happy on my own. I know I keep telling you all, but it's *huge* for me and for you to understand the importance of this. Nobody can make you happy other than yourself. I know that my Prince is on his way, from where, who knows? The point is I am in a good place so I know when he finally makes an appearance I will be ready with an open heart, sense of humor, and enough confidence to weather anything. I also know that I will not go back to "drama!" Love is supposed to feel good, not hurt. Relationships take work, yes, but not too much work.

Nowadays when I feel the slightest hint of negative thoughts coming on, I turn them around. I will not spend time thinking about "what ifs" anymore because deep down inside I just know. I know that some weekends are tough, especially some of the summer ones (with my daughter away at camp), but it won't last forever and it gives me time to work on my book and do anything else I feel like doing.

I love my new home and can't wait until it is completely done. Picking everything out myself is a lot of work, but so much fun. This home is mine and all about my kids and me. My room is set up with my wish boards and candles and a brand-new bed and sheets and there are always white or light pink roses next to my bed, they remind me of love.

I went to the beach this weekend with friends and I had fun. It's all in your attitude. We got a late start and didn't leave until 12:00 p.m. On the way to the Turnpike, guess who I passed? Mr. X. The wild part is in the morning I thought, *Maybe my friend will meet Mr. X. today.* There's always a possibility that we could bump into him, and there he was. I was kind of relieved that he was around this weekend. I guess he's not on some deserted island with a girl! Maybe he is just laying low like I am and trying to get his life back together. I hope so. I'm always rooting for the underdog!

In the mean time, RI is MIA again. He comments on my Facebook and says, "let's do NYC soon" but soon could mean another five years. He has had plenty of time to come see me. Sometimes we have people all wrong. I see exactly why he is still single and it's his choice, but I thought we would see each other by now. Maybe we will, but not until he is ready. I do have a sixth sense about things and I just can't see never seeing him again. Oh well life goes on. I think his new nickname will be "Big." (as in Sex in the City).

The most important thing is my happiness. I am in the midst of transition. I am setting up my home, preparing for the next phase of my life. My kids are doing really well; they love the new home. Everything is new and fresh and they know I am happy and that is huge. Sometimes I cry, but they help me like I help them. We have been through a lot and now with my parents being separated it's tough sometimes, but all in all we are moving forward to a better life. It's really hard with my mom being so depressed. If I wasn't doing so well, I do not think I would be able to handle it, but life happens for a reason and I am trying to help her understand that. How can a seventy-something woman who was married for fifty years understand that? Her generation was so different. If you were married, that was it for life for the most part. Even if you did not communicate or show any affection toward each other, you were married for life. I think my generation is suffering hugely because of this. So many of us grew up in unhappy houses and repeated the pattern for lack of knowing any better. Some of us do the same thing and stay unhappy. The lucky ones who have a strong foundation and still love each other have grown together and if need be they work on the relationship and go to counseling, therapy, etc. Then there are the ones who know there is something not right and the only chance they have of true happiness is to take a chance and be alone and maybe one day meet their next soul mate (hello).

I say NEXT *soul mate* because even though we may be divorced, and some of us are not even speaking to ex-spouses, we all know at one time our ex was our soul mate. Sometimes a soul mate is meant to teach us painful lessons, but they are still soul mates. If we weren't married to these people, we would not have learned the lessons or have our children, nor would we have had the chance to transform our lives. Everything in life is a lesson and a blessing. When you learn to look at life this way, it becomes less painful and more joyful. You cannot possibly waste time regretting or thinking about what you "should" have done. Here is one more thing I have learned the hard way: the scarier something is to do, the better the outcome.

I believe that marriage is going to come back in fashion again and be better than ever. I believe those of us who have gone through divorces are going to lead the way, if we take the time to figure out who we are first and not run desperately from one relationship to the next to avoid being alone. Being alone is what makes you appreciate new connections. I look forward to whatever is coming next; I know it is going to be different from my first marriage because I am different.

If I were to be totally honest with you, I would say I really never had a relationship as the confident, secure girl I am now. I think there was so much going on in my home when I was growing up that I repeated patterns and ran to guys as an escape or to be loved. I don't think I even thought twice about what was good for me. I just wanted to have boyfriends and I did. Now that I have figured out who I am and what I want, I don't have to look for it because it already lives inside of me. I can go to my romantic, happy place whenever I want, even if I am alone. I have learned to love myself so I don't feel a lack of love. I have been warming up my love muscles and thoughts for over a year now so I know when I feel that connection with someone again it will be magical. I am not scared it won't happen, nor am I scared of when it does. I know I will give it my all and let myself love again without holding back. After all that I have been through, if I have to play games and not express true love, then I know it isn't the right thing for me. The point is that I am confident enough now to know that I am enough. I don't have to be anything other than who I am and if it works, great, if not, I move on. When you are happy on your own, you open up to an entirely new world and see things with different eyes.

"T"

This "T" thing started when my publicist and I were brain storming one day about how I could coach a "player". After dealing with a few myself (ya' think?), I decided that I wanted to help these guys. I know most of you are thinking, *Why help these assholes?* I have a different perspective on it. Yes, some of them might be unworthy, but I, the hopeless romantic, believe that some of them are just insecure and have suffered the pain of failed relationships somewhere along the way (whether with their own marriages or relationships with their parents). I decided if I could get my hands on one who is willing to be coached, I would do it for free. I knew if I got into the head of one of these guys I could blog about it and help women and men understand the way they think, and eventually I could begin coaching men. Since my publicist is thirty-something, she has friends who are "playing" the field and she came up with "T." She said he would be perfect. He's funny (huge plus), good looking (uh oh), and willing and able (the deal breaker)!

T and I were introduced through email. We started with an interview. I emailed him a list of questions and when I got the responses I laughed so hard I was crying. This was going to be my biggest challenge yet. *Bring it on!* You can read the interviews on my website www.andrealifestylecoach.com on my blog page. I call it, "Beauty and the Beast." I read each answer and responded with my coaching tips and my sense of humor, which he inspired. *Okay, this was going to be fun!*

A few weeks after the interview, T mentioned he was coming to NYC to see his friends and do some business and we "flirted" with the fact that maybe we would meet in person. Well, we did and we had fun. If it was a date, it would have been my best one yet. We talked and laughed for hours; it was just easy. You all know I have a thing for guys who have a great sense of humor! It was business and I had to be mature about it. He is also a friend of my publicist. Anyway, my son called during our "meeting" because he was locked out of the new house and I had to leave very abruptly. T was not happy to say the least. I think T was thinking this was going to be another *Prince of Tides!*

The wild thing is that when I got home, I went to my room and I looked at my wish board and there was a picture of Vince Vaughan on it. T looks and acts exactly like him. Before we met I told T that I was writing a book that I hope to be a movie one day and he told me if he makes it in the movie he wants Vince Vaughn to play him! It's amazing how these things happen to me.

Anyway I told my publicist that I wanted out of the project because T was hitting on me and if he wasn't going to take this seriously, I was out. He ended up apologizing. He said he was just disappointed that I left! I know I am coaching *him*, but I have to admit he is teaching me also. He is teaching me how to laugh again! He even (after obviously reading my blogs) said to me, "Cinderella has to try on different shoes before she finds the right fit." We are still working together and flirting in between, he makes me laugh more than anyone ever has. He is so much fun and says it like it is. Stay tuned to more on "T."

Today I was flying home from Maine after visiting my daughter at camp and I said to my son, "I know what my movie is going to be about. Not only is it going to be a love story but I think it is going to be about me coaching a player and changing his life. I told him about T and how he makes me laugh. I think it was the first time I was able to talk to my son about me and another man without him getting upset. It's a sign! My kids know that I love funny people and it would make them happy if one day I had one in my life. (In real life, when you're divorced with kids, it's a package deal.) What a great story. I could end up changing someone's life and he could change mine. I already know that I want to meet a man who is fun, funny and easy going. I also need him to be in a great place. I was watching all of these couples this weekend at visiting day and some you can tell are just so bored and sick of each other, but then there are others who I envy. The ones who look at each other like they love each other and as I listen to them talk to each other there is a state of calmness, friendship, and respect that I love to hear. I don't get jealous when I see this, it just gives me hope.

I cannot forget the fact that T is a player but I can learn from him. I can learn how to play back and not take everything so seriously. I asked him the other day to find me someone just like him and he said he was sad I was giving up on him but he would try. Sometimes if you can really get to know a guy, you can see if he is capable of letting his guard down. Besides a little flirting can go a long way for your spirit. Not every guy is a potential husband but we can all learn from each other.

We all know I have dealt with a few players and one thing I know is when they stop communicating, get out quick! I know myself well enough to know I don't like waiting to hear from someone. On the same note, when we get a quick text, that is just a player's way of "keeping you around." I want to be with a guy who makes me laugh *but* contributes a helluva lot more to the relationship. One of the sexiest qualities a guy can have along with a sense of humor is the maturity to be with one woman. I also love when a guy thinks you are hot and sexy and he tells you. I love when I get the answers to the interview from T and it starts with, "read below hot stuff." It's so great to know that a guy thinks you are hot, it's empowering and boosts the confidence, which sometimes we all forget about.

When T and I first met I had to keep my composure, it was business and I also have a rule about first dates, or first coaching sessions (ha-ha). However, I am currently reading *The Vortex* by Jerry Hicks about the law of attraction and in it he says that we have to honor what our body wants on a physical level and not worry so much about the outcome. He said we have to give in to what our physical self wants in order to be authentic. Good thing I read this after meeting T! Or I should say I wish I had read it before?

We don't always know what to do. We always want to do the "right" thing, and sometimes we have these urges that we can't act on because our heads get in the way. I am not saying we should just jump into bed with anyone we meet, but when you are with a guy you just met and the conversation runs smoothly and comfortably and you feel good *and* you really do just want to kiss him—maybe you should. This is why I say he is teaching me as much as I am teaching him—just don't tell him! Maybe these players know something we don't, or maybe I know myself too well. Maybe there is another T coming along who is ready and stable. Sorry "T." Maybe he will make me laugh, call/text every day, be mature and emotionally available, and then I will feel comfortable about opening my heart and letting go again.

SHOULD I OR SHOULDN'T I

A week before "T" was coming to NYC again he made a huge Facebook announcement to whoever wanted to make plans. (Not arrogant, is he?) His post read, "coming to NYC next week if haven't already made plans with you, ping me." Anyway, I decided to play with him and responded with a text that read, "Ping!" So he called me Saturday night before his flight and we decided to see each other on Monday. I was really looking forward to it but wasn't sure I should. (With guys like this, do you ever really know? You can only play if your intent is to have fun.)

Monday I'm going about my day looking forward to hearing from him, he's so much fun! At 3:00 he calls from his parents'. He is leaving for the city soon and plans on seeing me around eight. Cool! I am looking forward to just hanging out with him, casual. I even told him just jeans. We planned to have a drink at his brother's apartment and then go for sushi. I was running late and he kept texting to see where I was. I think we were both really looking forward to seeing each other. It was nice. We already met so there was no pressure. We also had cyber space contact for the last three months.

I finally got to the apartment and he was making drinks and as soon as we saw each other it was just so comfortable. He is so funny, we just talked and laughed. I was so comfortable I even took off my uncomfortable heels. There was no reason to go anywhere. It was just great to hang out with someone laughing on the couch. I did get on his case a lot about the "player" nonsense on his Facebook. We are just two of the most completely opposite human beings, which made it even more fun. He is the perfect example of a player and I am so not. However—and here is the clincher—both are open to learning from each other. Here I was not knowing what to expect and not really thinking about it or caring . . . I was living in the moment. I was completely myself and so was he. I asked him if his parents knew he was seeing me tonight—a normal, Jewish, 49 year old mother of 3, stable girl. He said, "If they did, they would be shining the shoes and getting the tuxedo out!"

Anyway, one thing led to another and before I knew it . . . (being the lady that I am I will leave out the details and leave them for your imagination, but it felt damn good to let it all go and just have fun). I felt sexy and alive for the first time in years! I had my mojo back. There wasn't any relationship drama. We were friends having fun . . . *allowed*!

I waited until my forties to do what most of my friends were doing in college and after college when I had the responsibility of owning a children's clothing store *and* was in an on again off again relationship with my ex-husband. So while all my peers were all out sowing their oats, I had responsibilities and other things on my mind. This was my night to have fun and let it go and not care about tomorrow, and I had the perfect partner.

Later "T" mentioned that he got us food. He took out forks and we ate shrimp salad and mozzarella and tomatoes from deli containers! I never laughed so much! It really turned out to be a great night. It's not about where you go or what you do; it's just about having a good old-fashioned time. I know this will not be my usual MO. I like being in a relationship and if I could have this much fun with someone who is also emotionally ready and stable it would be amazing. (That is what I am going to have!) On my way home, he texted, "Focus on the road and stop thinking about me!" I just laughed. I finally had a fun night. I never would have even met him if it weren't for my coaching business. Like I have been saying all along, online dating is not the answer for everyone. I will continue to "do my thing" knowing it will bring me more fun nights and eventually . . . true love.

If you have strict morals, that's okay; I do as well. However, there is nothing wrong with having a little bit of fun in life as long as you use protection! I am not referring to condoms here, although they are a *must*. I am referring to protecting your heart. If you have worked on yourself as much as I have, then you have developed a strong core. Once you have that strong core and confidence, you can make choices and do things without worrying about getting hurt or about the outcome. So having a few fun nights can't hurt!

GETTING A BAND-AID
CAN GIVE YOU HOPE

I never knew starting over in my new home could feel like this. I wish you all could come visit my new home, it is *me*. It's filled with roses and candles and it's modern, sleek and homey. My friend said to me today that I am "getting everything in place for what is coming." I know she was talking about Prince whoever, but part of me feels like it's already here. Just the sheer joy of creating my own environment for me and my kids is . . . *priceless!* My home is a total reflection of my dreams. I could never live any other way again. There is no clutter, no junk closets or drawers, no unnecessary "stuff" in our lives anymore.

Even though I am really happy, I still have a few hours or two throughout my day when I feel painfully alone. I never feel like I will be alone forever like I did when I was first divorced. Sometimes it gets hard and I am still a little confused when it comes to men, but as I become more confident and more myself, I feel more optimistic.

I love little moments of faith and hope. Today I was running around New York City in the pouring rain in heels and I got the worst blister.I could hardly walk so I ran into a deli to get some fresh roses and hopefully Band-Aids. I practically kissed the poor Korean owner when I saw that he sold them. I tore open the box and quickly began to put on a Band-Aid before even paying and as I stood up I came face to face with one of the most gorgeous faces I have ever seen. I swear this man looked exactly like one of the guys on my wish board. He was around forty, dressed super cool, and carrying Louis Vuitton shopping bags. I thought *Wow, a cool guy who knows how to shop, who is breathtakingly beautiful.* We had a flirty moment with smiles and blushes and he kept coming back to the counter to smile at me. I was late for my next client and didn't really know what to do when all of a sudden the movie *Serendipity* came to mind. I realized it was a sign; it was a sign to leave now and just be glad that God gave me a sign today that what I want is out there. Who knows? Maybe I will see this guy again and we will bump into each other when it is right. The point is it gave me hope. The main thing is I am in a good place right now and thinking positively. (and next time I pass a Louis Vuitton store I will make sure to check it out)!

When I finally got into bed that night I must admit I was thinking (fantasizing) about Mr. Louis Vuitton.I think it is important for all women married or single to experiment with their sexuality.So many married people go such long periods of time without having sex. I think the more you experiment with yourself, the easier it is to jumpstart the desires that have been buried away under the routine of daily living, Besides, it makes you feel sexy and alive and that is what inspires your mate. Turn yourself on and it will turn him on. Rather than nag, complain, and blame him for the lack of sex, do something to change the situation. This is true with everything in life. "Be the change you want to see". Your happiness is your own responsibility, it is not anyones job to make you happy. Live by this rule and everyone around you will be happier.

IT TOOK VIRAL MENINGITIS
TO BUMP INTO MR. X

As my BFFs say, "You couldn't make this stuff up." My daughter and I get home from taking my oldest son back to college in Arizona and my other son is lying on the couch not feeling well. He feels warm, has a headache and sore throat so I tell him to "get into bed and I will call the doctor in the morning." A few hours later his neck is really hurting and right away I think, *Oh shit. Meningitis.* I call my pediatrician. He's away and the hospital calls me back to say if he can't sleep come to the emergency room, otherwise go to the doctor in the morning. He falls asleep finally and I am up all night. I am tired, still on Arizona time and worrying if I am doing the right thing by not going right to the hospital. I keep going to my sons room to feel his head but he seems okay. Times like this you only have your own parental instincts.

Fast-forward to the doctor's office. I take him to my doctor who looks at him and sends us right to the ER. At this point I am panicking. I call my ex and we meet with the neurologist who suggests a spinal so they can test the fluid to see if it's viral or bacterial meningitis—bacterial is deadly without antibiotics; viral just takes time to heal. Let's not even go into the fact that my ex, my son, and I were in a room together that was the size of my bathroom for several hours. Times like these you just have to rise to the occasion and suck it up and act like human beings for the sake of your kids. No matter how much you dislike each other, you both love your kids. I did realize sitting there that I have really come a long way and am no longer emotionally attached to him at all—*yay!* Sometimes being around him triggers the fear I used to have, before understanding his pain and anger, but now I can talk myself through it.

The neurologist comes back and says we have to leave the room for half an hour during the spinal. Since I haven't eaten all day, I decided to run to this Italian market that makes chopped salads and the ex wants a coffee. (Sure dear, anything else while I'm out?) So I get to the market and I see Mr. X's car. I am so stressed and worried at this point I run in like a tornado, rushing to get back to my son, and he is sitting at a table with his son, looking damn good. He says, "Nice parking job." (Shit, he broke the ice.) I say, "I'm totally flipping out right now." He says, "Why?" and I just start rambling, not thinking about how I haven't heard from him in so long but I am not angry. I am just being honest to goodness me. There was something very real and soothing about talking to him. I told him about my son and at the same time I am ordering a salad and kidding around with the counter guys. (They know me at this place; I'm the "salad girl.") It became very comical. I yelled over to the drink counter that I needed a coffee with milk. They are all laughing, saying, "You drink green tea. What's the deal?" I say it's for the ex, have you ever? the nerve of him? The guy says, "With sugar?" and I say "I honestly can't remember. Married for twenty years and I can't remember". At this point the whole place is laughing! They ask me if I am going to the pet store next (it's next door and I always used to get Jack cookies and treats there) and I scream, "Pet store? Don't you remember my dog died in April?" Mr. X (who is a dog person) says, "You're kidding. What happened?" So, I told him my Jack story. I look him right in the eye and say from my gut holding my hand on my heart, "It was the worst day of my life. I totaled the car on the way to the vet." Everyone is shocked and still laughing. I say, "It has been the worst year . . . but I am still standing!" Mr. X wants to know if my son is going to be okay and I say I don't know but I hope so and leave quickly.

When I finally get into my car I call my three BFFs and they are freaking out because I finally saw him and spoke to him. In the back of my mind I thought maybe I would hear from him, either a call or a text just to see how my son is, but no. It makes me realize, *Could I ever care for a man who doesn't even call to see about my kid? No.* It's okay though. My standards have gone up after spending all of this time alone. I would never settle for someone who wouldn't call. It only shows me that the best is yet to come and no, Mr. X is not the finale. It took me almost four years to realize that, but it's okay. Look how much has changed and happened to me in that time. I am a different person living in a different home with a different life.

CLOSURE

I decided for my fiftieth birthday I would send Mr. X an email. I had to express to him how painful it was to never have heard from him again. I didn't do this for a response, I did it for myself. In my coaching practice, I always have my clients express their feelings to someone who has hurt them, so they can move on. I have learned with relationships that the pain and the hanging on tortures us because there either isn't any closure. After a certain amount of time, and when you learn how to not care about the outcome, I say go for it, put it in writing. Get those feelings out of your body and make room for the right soul mate. He can't enter your life until the old "stuff" is gone. It won't work.

Anyway, I sent an email thanking him for being there for me when I had my surgery, when my grandmother died, and for making me realize I was worth a lot more than I thought. I expressed how painful it was to never have heard from him after he at one time led me to believe he wanted to be with me. I won't go into too much detail because for whatever reason he ran away is really his issue and not mine. I do wish him well and feel sorry for him. Hating him and being angry would only affect my well–being, and I don't have time for that . . . I am preparing for my real "soul mate." He was not the reason I left my marriage but he did help wake me up as did RI.

RI called me! I looked at my cell and couldn't believe it. I was so happy to hear from him. He was in South Beach, of course two weeks after I told him I'd be there, but I admit I was really happy. RI is a different kind of Mr. X, I know if I really need him I can call and he'll be there.

RI PUTS IT IN PERSPECTIVE

You are not going to believe this. I have to move because my landlord is moving into this townhouse *and* my ex is taking me to court to redo our agreement. So not only do I have nowhere to live come this summer, I don't know what my finances will be. I also don't know if I want to live in this town anymore. It will only be my daughter and I next year and she is open to a big change. I have to decide if we are going to start over some place or stay where we are. So I would say there is a lot on my plate.

I texted RI to tell him I'm having a hard time and wanted to say hi. I went to sleep feeling drained from the week but determined to get up and go to Soulcycle and clear my head. No matter what happens, you still have to look (and feel) good!

I came home, took a shower, and when I looked at my cell phone I saw RI called! Wow! Two phone calls in two weeks. Maybe we are finally making some progress. I love talking to him; he gives good phone! Anyway, I told him why I am having a hard time and he said his week wasn't so great either—he hurt his neck at the gym and had an MRI and they found a lump on his thyroid. He is having it removed and biopsied in Boston this week. My heart sank, but I kept it together. Please, God, let him be okay. It certainly put life into perspective for me. I also wondered how he could listen to me complaining about my "stuff "and give me advice when he has something serious to deal with . . . because he's a good guy. I don't know what will be with him and me. I do know that sometimes when you give people space and let things happen organically, they can turn out good. I like him a lot and no matter what happens . . . always will. He likes me too. And . . . like is a really great place to be right now.

HOW I GOT HERE

I think it's important to keep updating you on my life so you know how far I have come. I know some of you have no clue how to even get started with your new journey and aren't even sure if you are ready for one at all. There are a few things that really helped me that I constantly work on with my clients as well. The first and most important is your mind-set; learning how to change negative thoughts and feelings into positive ones. I've learned the hard way that the only opinion that counts is your own. There are many toxic, unhappy people out there who have never dealt with their own "stuff. These people find pleasure in hurting and insulting others. This is really their own misery being projected onto you. People who have low self-esteem and confidence issues will do whatever they can to make others feel as badly as they do.

When you regain your confidence, the people in your life will change. When you feel good about yourself, you want to be around the same. You will also "magnetize" and attract loving, fun, supportive people. This is very true when it comes to your love life as well. Sometimes we tolerate abuse when we aren't sure of ourselves. Sometimes we feel this is the best we can do. *Not true*. Do the work. I guarantee it changes your life forever. Being confident and loving yourself is the key to happiness. It isn't about finding the right guy/girl; it's really about finding yourself. The sooner you understand that, the better your love life will be (whether you are single or married).

I coach both married and single people. I think most marriages fail because people aren't happy with themselves and tend to blame their spouses. The first step in finding out is to work on your self. I did a lot of self-work and worked with therapists and eventually a life coach before I made my decision to leave my marriage. Working with a coach helped make it clearer to me what I wanted. I sort of knew in the back of my mind but I needed to break down many layers of built-up fear. It took digging deep to get me to move way forward. Once you learn how to let the past go, your life begins to move ahead. I took slow baby steps at first, but now I am able to take giant leaps. I have my confidence and my dignity back and no one will ever take that from me. Once you find it, you have it forever.

I have come to realize and accept the fact that I am who I am. The only way I can be a loving mom and soul mate to someone is if I can be the real me. If I want to cleanse, sleep naked, get my hair blown out, buy a new dress, be a lifestyle coach, give my kids advice on sex and partying instead of lecturing them as if I was never in their shoes, buy my food at Whole Foods, dress like I'm from LA without anyone criticizing, abusing, controlling, or putting me down (get the picture?) then so be it. It just means I have my own way of doing things.

I think between suburbia and marriage it is possible to really lose your own identity. Sometimes I would be at the supermarket and get this sick feeling in my gut. I felt somehow I was giving up on myself and my dreams. I knew I had so much more to offer but I had no idea what it was. Every week it was a new diet, new gym, new advice book, or new makeup, but nothing was really turning me on. I always loved volunteering and helping people but I wanted a career, I wanted to do something where I could incorporate the real me and "my message" to others. I began to realize no matter what I wore or how I did my hair, I had this inner sadness that could not be covered by even the best makeup artist. And believe me; I tried them all!

I didn't know who I was or what to do with my life. I felt like I was being who others wanted me to be. I felt suppressed and phony for not standing up for myself. Yes, I was a wife and a mom of three kids, but it wasn't enough. I wasn't being challenged or inspired to be myself. Little by little I taught myself how. I always knew I had a sixth sense when it came to giving people advice. I was always good at helping people with business advice as well, even though I am not a "corporate" person in any way. I always loved giving relationship advice too, but I was giving it to everyone but myself. I never wanted to hurt anyone but I realized I was hurting them by pretending I was happy

LESSONS FROM RI

I have learned to be patient and let life evolve the way it's supposed to. It's different with RI, he is one of the reasons I have this new life and have written this book. People come into our lives for different reasons and maybe he and I haven't figured that one out yet, but I will always be grateful for him being in this world. I think we often have a struggle between our minds and our hearts. If I was just using my head, I would tell myself not to speak to him since he won't see me, but in real life I don't really feel that way. My heart says something different. We never really know what is going on in someone else's life and being angry only makes us feel (and look) bad.

Timing plays a huge role in life. Instead of thinking maybe he just isn't ready, I wonder sometimes if maybe it's me who isn't ready. I do agree to work on loving yourself and not to push for a relationship, and I don't see anything wrong with reaching out to RI to say hi. I don't expect anything from him and respect the space right now. It's so rare to have a special connection with someone; we all need that. It doesn't always have to be marriage or commitment; sometimes it can be someone who lives three states away. So don't write people off too quickly if you aren't getting the results you want. Just go about your life and time will tell if you are supposed to be together in the long run. This is why it is so important to do the work and get to a place where you are confident and secure with yourself and not depending on other people for your happiness. If I was depending on RI and a relationship with him, I would be a mess. I have total faith in myself and God to know things will work out for me the way they are supposed to, and for him as well.

I emailed RI the other night because I got great responses from two editors about this book and thanked him because he has been such a special part of this journey. His response, written to "Princess" (love that), made me smile and ended with "talk soon." He once told me that he's the one who discovered me. I loved the way he put that. He's the one who helped me discover myself. Although I had to stay away from him out of respect for my marriage, I'll never forget sitting by myself one night in South Beach crying into my hands because, even though I was confused and scared, someone had touched my soul and made me realize how special I was. He made me feel like I was alive again. Yes, I was discovered. He brought out the best in me without me doing anything but being myself. I was never the same after my cry that night. I was broken open. It was such fate that he was just sitting at a pool one day, newly divorced. Thank you God, for creating that scenario, your timing was perfect. I can't wait to see more of your work! (LOL)

Sometimes I think about the day when we can see each other face to face. I think it will make me cry. I have traveled a long, hard road since that weekend in South Beach. I have had many ups and downs. What gets me through it all is knowing I never have to pass up an RI again because I am now free to love whoever I want. I know it has to be a fun, loving, stable, and sexy relationship because that is the only way it will work for me. I have learned so much about myself through RI. I hope reading this book brings him as much happiness as it did for me to write it. We have already discussed it and he already "loves his chapter."

MANIFESTING

I am here to tell all of you that even though divorce happens, dogs die, friends die, tumors are removed, parents divorce, the economy worsens, and kids grow up and go to college, we can go through it all, keep our heads held high, and come out on the other side. I have to tell you that it does not matter who filed for divorce or who left who. A failed marriage is just as painful for *both* parties. Just because one of you made the decision it doesn't mean it is any easier for the other person. Even though I *had* to let myself grow, the growing pains were very real. I still have them sometimes but they are not as severe as they used to be. I have trained myself to cry when I need to rather than keep it in.

I want you all to understand that it is possible to change how you feel about yourself. It's possible to grow up feeling insecure about your looks, your body, and your personality even though everything seems to be alright on the outside. You can function and work, get married, and have children, but it's not until you are ready to really face yourself that life changes. True beauty comes out only when it is felt within and that isn't BS! Nobody loves having their hair and makeup done or having a photo shoot more than I do, but that took years of hard work. I had to love my inner self to be able to show it to a camera. Having photos taken has been very therapeutic for me. Each time I have Laura Bruen (www.laurabruen.com) shoot me, I am in a different place in my life. This summer I am having boudoir photos done! No, it's hardly *Playboy*, but it is one of my goals for myself and a gift for my future soul mate. Since beginning this journey, the stakes have gotten higher, but I keep getting better . . . and so will you.

My life has completely changed and that is the beauty of growth and allowing things to happen without predicting any outcomes. I have learned to be patient and not to pursue anyone or any relationship and when someone comes forward instead of getting crazy and planning the fantasy wedding in my head, I "lean back" (a phrase my clients hear me say *all* the time). You lean back a little and enjoy every second of the moment. Do not think about one hour or one minute past where you are or you will miss it! So many of us are so wrapped up in the "what's going to happen" that we miss out on what is right in front of us. If you learn to live like this, love and relationships are lighter, more fun, and eventually much deeper. Allowing yourself to fall in love slowly is the most intense, gratifying experience, and this is coming from someone who used to be the one leaning forward! I had to continue my journey on my own, out of a marriage that I outgrew, in order to find my true self, knowing someday it would lead me to my next soulmate.

It took a long time, a lot of heartache and many lonely nights to get here, but I would do it all over again to get where I am right now; sitting in my new home, in my new kitchen, wearing a sexy little black dress, feeling radiant and lucky enough to be a lifestyle coach and help other people get here too. Yes, I would do it again in a heartbeat. Who knows what life will bring, what joys, and what hardships? If I can be this happy after what I have been through, then so be it!

I totally believe in manifesting your dreams. I believe you can have anything and everything you want. You might fall on your face many times until you get there, but that's life and anyway what's the hurry?

151

When you manifest, you take your dreams one step further. Instead of "wishing" you begin "knowing." You know in your soul that it will all happen at the right time so instead of dreading the time, parties, weddings, and weekends you spend alone, you prepare and look forward to what is coming. Manifesting is about living "as if" it has already happened. Be excited just knowing even though it might not all be here yet, it's just a matter of time, and the universe is taking care of it. You have nothing to worry about. Your job is to be patient, be positive, and be ready. As far as love goes, there is nothing that will stop you and your soul mate from being together. As far as work goes, whatever you want to do, just do it. Go for it. Try it. Lastly, as far as your dream body goes, that is just a matter of loving yourself enough to treat your body well with healthy food and exercise. All of this comes down to self-esteem and having confidence in yourself. You break through the layers of doubt, fear, and insecurity and *everything* about your life changes for the better. This is what I do in my coaching practice. No matter what reason a client starts working with me, after a few sessions they not only feel better but they start to look better as well. They are more relaxed and more comfortable being themselves with me and eventually they start being more authentic in their day to day lives. When you feel better on the inside it shows on the outside.

I can give my clients inner and outer beauty tips but happiness looks prettier than any makeup. I can recommend the perfect lip gloss but it only looks great on a smile. You can count on Botox (nothing wrong with it) but with less stress and anxiety you won't need as much. This is why I am a lifestyle coach and not just life coach. First, I help my clients get their confidence and self esteem back and then we have fun enhancing it!

I have two wish boards hanging in my bedroom. They literally took two years to complete. Creating them was one of the first steps I took to manifest my next love. I also light my candles around my bathtub and as I lie in the bathtub I light one for my kids, one for my work, one for my family, and one for my soul mate. I light one for my soul mate so he can continue his journey and find his way to me. These are just a few of the rituals I practice that have changed the way I look at my life.

Although I do take care of myself physically with facial acupuncture, exercise, eating healthy, great hair people at Oscar Blandi, love having my makeup done and doing photo shoots, it is my inner strength and confidence that outweigh it all. When you feel good about yourself, you can put on sweatpants and no makeup and go out feeling good, but don't! As I wrote in one of my many "inner beauty" blogs—always look presentable and *never* go out without lip gloss! Ironically, what happens is when you begin to feel alive and confident, you want to show the world how great you feel. I think I look better now than I did ten years ago and if the hundreds of emails I get on dating sites from guys in their thirties is any indication, the proof is in the pudding. Mind you, I am not a cocky person at all but after going through so much and turning a lot of lemons into lemonade, it makes me feel pretty good.

Every woman out there has an inner diva and the ability to look hot, sexy, and beautiful. When you learn (with the right tools) how to peel away the layers of self-doubt, it begins to emerge. There is no reason for anybody to feel less worthy than anyone else. It makes me so sad when I see women who have chosen to let themselves go. One of my favorite things to watch is a makeover show; Oprah used to have them all the time. I would cry my eyes out like a baby seeing how someone was transformed! This is what I do with my clients, whether they have relationship, weight, or career issues. I know they are on the road I took and I am going to pull them along until they are completely transformed, happy, and confident. I know their careers will get better, their homes will reflect their new confidence, they will get into awesome shape, and they will look and feel younger, stronger, and sexier than ever. It's all about confidence. I am really a "confidence coach." I can see the potential in everyone I meet. When I get *them* to believe in themselves, big things happen.

I learned to love myself first and that is the only way I can truly love someone else at this level. I have lived through some very difficult times and I have waited for my soulmate to love himself, so he can fully love me. We both love ourselves and our love for each other is a potent combination (mentally and physically).

GROWING UP

How did I become fifty? I think because I feel so young at heart it's hard to believe. I look at it as if the second half of my life is now beginning. It's all in the way we think about things. I know a lot of women who are fifty+ and I have to say I have never seen such a diverse group. Some listen to the "rules schmules" and cut their hair and stop wearing sexy clothes and then there is Madonna, Demi Moore, Michelle Pfeifer need I say more?

From forty-five to fifty I felt like I went through twenty years of change. I am still in the process. I think even though change is scary and really hard, we always have to be in the changing and growing process, at least some of us do. Being stagnant and resisting change is mediocre and boring. If you don't open your eyes and your world to new things and new people, you will be missing so much. It is also so important to be with someone who is open to change and growth so you can get to the next stage together.

This is true with exercise and eating habits as well. You have to change it up. I use to only run until I took a class at Soulcycle. I couldn't believe I could get the runner's high and at the same time be singing my heart out and working on my arms! My back pain went away and my knees feel like I had them replaced! You never really know until you try.

My views and feelings about marriage have changed drastically. I am still a hopeful romantic and believe in marriage and weddings, but I believe strongly in writing your own vows. I think every couple is unique and on your special wedding day you should share your special story with everyone.. I am very big on hearing people's stories. I like to know how people met and when and how they knew they found "the one." I love to see older couples who are still looking into each other's eyes. I love to see couples laughing and holding hands. I just love LOVE.

I have this letter hanging on my wish board, I read it every night before I go to sleep. It's from God.

Dear One,

Everyone longs to give himself or herself completely to someone, to have a deep soul relationship with another, to be loved thoroughly and exclusively, but I say "No." Not until you are satisfied, fulfilled, and content with being alone, with giving yourself totally and unreservedly to Me, will you be ready to have the intensely personal and unique relationship that I have planned for you. You will never be united with anyone or anything else until you are united with Me. I want you to stop planning, stop wishing, and start allowing Me to give you the most thrilling plan in existence – one that you cannot even imagine. I want you to have the best. Please, allow Me to bring it to you.

You must keep watching Me expecting the greatest of things. Keep experiencing the satisfaction that I AM. Keep listening and learning the things that I will tell you. Just wait. That's all. Don't be anxious. Don't worry. Don't look around at the things others have or that I have given them. Don't look at the things you think you want. Just keep looking up to Me or you will miss what I want to show you. And then, when you are ready, I will surprise you with a love far more wonderful than any you have dreamed of.

You see, until you are ready and until the one I have for you is ready (I am working even at this moment to have you both ready at the same time), until you are both satisfied exclusively with me and the life I have prepared for you, you won't be able to experience the love that exemplifies your relationship with Me. This is Perfect Love.

And Dear One, I want you to have this most wonderful love. I want to see in the flesh a picture of your relationship with Me, and to enjoy materially and concretely the everlasting union of beauty, perfection, and love that I offer. Know that I love you utterly. Believe it and be satisfied.

Love,
God

MY MIRACLE

I decided to take my daughter to LA for a weekend; it's our favorite place to shop and eat. It gave us something to look forward to. I decided to book flights from LGA instead of Newark for a little change. I have "bicoastal" on my wish board, not that I am planning anything but, if Mr. Bicoastal is traveling this week he will be leaving from NYC and not Newark.

We get to the airport in the afternoon. I am feeling really good and my body is in good shape, which always makes me feel good. I have been super good with eating, cleansing, and spinning. I love wearing tank tops now and my hair is finally long!

We get through airport security and I spot a cute, cool guy. I assume he is going back to LA, his hair is not typical of a New Yorker. I wish I could live out there part time, just seeing these healthy looking men every day would be worth it. Anyway, I can't stop checking him out, he's too busy on his BlackBerry to notice so I'm having even more fun! He's laughing while talking on his cell—probably to his hot thirty-year-old girlfriend who looks like Jessica Biel. He has to be going to La La land because he is dressed that way: jeans, button-down shirt, and instead of the NYC "designer loafers" he's wearing really cute sneakers, a great looking Rolex, (Phew!) and a great leather jacket. Where are these guys in New York? I think in Tribeca . . . anyway, I am having fun watching him.

My daughter and I went to Starbucks, the bathroom, made a candy run and got to the gate just in time. He's there, in the first-class line. Is he too good to be true? He's probably a big time "player." All of a sudden he comes over to my daughter who thinks he is hot too and says, "Are you in line with your mom or your sister?" *Holy shit!* I think, *What a line, what a bummer. Why are the cute ones always players?* My daughter says, "She's my mom." I am standing right there, don't forget. He says, "Why are you going to LA?" My daughter says, "we like it there and it's my moms weekend." Ok, now he knows I'm divorced.

The line starts moving and he sits down in first class and says to my daughter, "Tell your mom I will come say hi later." I know I look good and I am so due for a great guy, but not another player, no way, no how. My daughter is already hooked, but I told her, "Once he has a drink and some real food up there, he will forget about us little people in the back." It's okay. I'm sure he has a girlfriend or twenty for that matter.

Sure enough, an hour into the flight, he comes walking down the aisle looking around. I was reading a magazine and look up into the most gorgeous, romantic eyes. He's that confident type that I like (which I am not sure is confidence or cockiness yet). He's being really funny and talking to all the people sitting near me. He's the type of guy who just makes you laugh! His delivery is quick. My heart is saying, *Stay away, girl!* He says to my daughter, "I'm sure your mom wants to take you for sushi tonight but will you give me her cell number so I can call you guys in the morning and maybe I can show you around LA?" I'm thinking, *Shoot, he must have a date tonight, or a wife, now I know he lives in LA.* My daughter gives him my number and he goes back to his seat.

He stays put for the rest of the flight and I am already assuming I will never hear from him and if he is a player that is fine. I did not come this far in my life to go backward. I have gotten rid of every bad relationship and spent time clearing the way for a good one. I have to stay open though. We get off the plane and he is nowhere in sight, probably making out with his twenty-something girlfriend already. We go to the baggage check and he's there with his bag and says, "Where have you been, we all have our luggage already." His delivery is so funny. He is pretending to yell at me like I am his wife and I say, "Spoken like a true husband." He turned red and we both laughed and he says, "Ya' think?" I'm dying and thinking, *Just go with it.*

He then leans over and whispers, "My name is Michael. I have been divorced for three years. I have three kids and I live in NYC downtown. I am renting a house in Santa Monica for the year because I am working on a film. I see my kids every other week and I might buy this house I am renting because I love it but I also have a house in East Hampton where I usually spend my summers. I know you probably think I am just another player because I am sure you get hit on constantly. I have had my share of flings but I am ready to move on with a cool girl. So if you want me to show you and your daughter some really cool stores and take you for a great lunch then answer your cell in the morning. I know you have been hurt, but we all have. I guarantee you will have fun with me. I have a sixteen-year-old daughter and a twenty-year-old son, I know the drill. I have to tell you before we go one step further—I also have an eight-year-old."

We both laughed and I looked him in the eye and said, "Pick us up at one o'clock at Shutters and if you are more than five minutes late, I will assume you are full of shit. Have a great night."

We get our luggage and rental car and we are hungry and tired. The plan is to drop our stuff at the hotel and go for a great dinner. I am so excited about Michael but I do not want to let my daughter know that, just in case. We go to Roku, our favorite Santa Monica sushi place. Thank God I am thin and can eat because I am so nervous and excited. (Please, please be real this time!) We order dinner and I get a text from an unfamiliar 917 number: "what kind of roll are you eating?" "who is this?" "Michael from the plane. How many 917s have your number?" "More than you can imagine LOL" "Have fun, I will text you before you go to bed *and* in the morning. Looking forward to seeing you guys." "me too."

For a split second the old me thinks, *what does this adorable guy want with me?* Immediately the *new* me thinks, *You are awesome, cool, hot, fun, funny, grounded, healthy, sweet, stable, secure . . . and ready—that's what!*

We get back to the room and my daughter falls asleep watching TV and Michael calls. I answer with "Good timing, she just fell asleep." "I figured that" he says. "So why is a girl like you still single?" "Don't start with those lines because this time I will end this before it gets started." He says, "I'm sorry but I just want to know about you." I say, "Ask me questions."

We talked for two hours. He made me laugh so much and said, "You should give me a chance, otherwise it could be a long, cold winter for you." I'm *dying*. We hang up and I try to fall asleep but it's impossible. Wow, is this it? Is this everything I have been dreaming about for four years? Are my single days over? Is it possible that I can really lean back and let this delicious man steer the boat for me? Is this the guy who has my back for the rest of my life? Can I relax into this feeling and not be afraid?

It's hard to trust after all I have been through with men, but what is different now is I trust myself. I know I don't have to try to make things work. I know if they are right they will work organically.

Three hours later I get a text, "I read your website . . . How would you like to write your next book on the beach at my house in East Hampton? I promise to leave you alone until 7:00 p.m. every day. However, at 7 you are all mine. I love to cook, or we can go out, your choice. I have a lot of fun friends so dinner parties are a must. You don't have to cook . . . just be my Princess. I know what you are thinking, not again with the lines, but Andrea, I have been waiting for you and I promise to prove it. Sweet dreams, see you in a few hours."

I can't ruin my next book but I will tell you this: do not ever settle or compromise on love. Whatever you are dreaming about, keep dreaming. I never would have made it this far without my dreams. I always had faith that one day it would all come together. I always believed in love at first site and no, you can't possibly know a person without spending time with them, but if your gut is telling you something then just go with it. If you don't open yourself up to love, even though sometimes it might be wrong and cause you pain, you will never know when it's right. I felt something in my heart the minute I met him . . . and so did he.

Love is a choice. You can choose to love each other and make it work. You can choose your own path. People ask me all the time about getting married again. Sometimes I think yes, definitely, but sometimes I say, "I love the Kurt and Goldie thing." I love when two people are together because they choose to be. If the door is open, you are there by choice not because of a piece of paper. I think that is so romantic. Sometimes I still dream about my next "beach" wedding so I haven't really decided. Why decide now? I like it so much better when things aren't planned.

To be continued . . . (Next book.)

CH CH CH CHANGES . . . .

By now I am sure you realize my story is not only about getting through a divorce, it's about learning about myself. Yes, divorce is about the painful break up of a family, but the most painful part for me has been the realization that if my childhood had been different and I valued myself more, I could have probably avoided a lot of pain in my life. What makes my life so great is knowing that I have learned to love myself and I am reinventing my life to be exactly what I knew it was meant to be. It's as if there was another person living inside of me who has broken out of her protective shell. Yes, I still have more to learn and I know I'll never stop growing nor let anyone stop me from being who I am. I have committed myself and my career to helping others find their confidence so they can live the life they are meant to live without being afraid. I hope to one day work with teenagers. I think the younger you learn self-esteem the better.

On a personal note, here are some differences in the way I live today compared to two years ago. When you emotionally detach from what others think and say about you,(and keep believing and knowing who you really are), you realize that people who cause you pain are only in pain themselves.

A huge step for me was learning to appreciate a Mr. X for what he is. You have to stop trying to make relationships happen and just "lean back" (my famous quote) and let them develop. If something doesn't feel right and it is hurting you, rather than force it, let it go. Clear the slate. If you are holding onto MAYBES, you will not be able to recognize what is right for you. It took me a long time to master this. I realized it's better for me to be open to something new than to spend my energy on "what should have been." The right guy/girl will find you at the right time. I believe this happens for everyone. There is nothing in the world that could keep your soul mate away from you!

Choosing love over fear is a huge step in transformation. Did you know in every situation in your life you have two choices: love or fear? It is also a choice whether you are going to be happy or depressed everyday. Unless you have clinical depression, it is that simple. When I wake up in the morning, I tell myself, "Anything can happen today" so why be miserable?" I have had many setbacks along the way but I have only gotten stronger and better in spite of it all.

My home is very close to what I dreamed it to be. It is calm and peaceful and filled with new things. My bedroom and bathroom are never without candles and roses nor are they every messy. I love every room in the house. There are no more junk drawers. I know where everything is and it is always clean. This home is mine and my kids'. We have made a new life here.

It is really hard for me having both sons away at college. I miss them terribly. They are both very protective of me, I am close to both of them.

People say my boys are like this because they know I am such a good mom and that makes me happy because we have been in some very tough situations. When going through my divorce I put my own needs aside for my kids. I literally made a pact with myself that I would stay home the first year until my kids were somewhat stable. I wanted them to always know I was home for them. Despite being ridiculed by a select few for being alone, I didn't care—my love life could wait. My kids came first.

I began to feel better and better about myself. My ex's opinions were affecting me less and less. As you feel better about yourself, the abuse lessens its grip and you begin to feel sorry for people knowing that they are projecting their own fears onto you. It is no longer my problem, it is only my responsibility to control my anger when I am being manipulated—and that has been my greatest challenge. My kids do not want to be in the middle or be involved no matter who is right or wrong. You have to just keep feelings to yourself and kids figure it out on their own.

People tell me what a great job I am doing with my kids all the time. They acknowledge how my strength is getting everyone through a really tough time. There were times I just wanted to give up I got so tired of it all, but I knew I was on the right road, and I was right!

The greatest thing that has come from my reinvention is this book and my coaching practice. I hope this book will be the first of many. I always knew my voice needed to be heard. I feel like I am saying the things some of you are thinking. I used to be afraid to express what I was thinking because of what others might think. Obviously that is no longer true. It's so rewarding when I post on my Facebook fan page and within hours I have comments and likes. I think that says it all. I will never keep my thoughts to myself again. I know my journey is helping others and I believe not saying how you feel causes anxiety, heartache, and makes you physically ill.

Living authentically and being true to who I am has made me feel beautiful. Beauty really does come from within. We can enhance our beauty but it only works if we feel good on the inside.When you have confidence, you can turn any head in a room. Getting divorced was really hard but as I began enjoying being "free", I began to feel prettier and prettier. I always exercised and ate healthy for the most part, but I began to take it to another level. I started weight lifting and toning.

I started taking spinning class in NYC, I started bimonthly facial acupuncture, and I started taking calcium, omega, and vitamin D. I trimmed my hair so I could have long, healthy hair again. I stopped wasting my days doing simple errands and began writing a book and working on my coaching practice. I stopped watching so much TV and began to read and write more. I filled my bathtub with candles. I framed two gorgeous wish boards with pictures and words about exactly what I wanted in a soul mate. I committed my time to myself and not to looking for a boyfriend.

HOW I FINALLY GOT TO MY HAPPY PLACE—(AND HOW YOU CAN TOO!)

Okay, so how did I get here? I got here by trial and error. I read and went to seminars and tried different techniques and ended up taking a little bit from different life coaches. I learned what works for me and what doesn't. From this realization I have created my own style of lifestyle coaching, which seems to be working really well. I have found my passion through my own transformation. I get so passionate coaching my clients. I love seeing them shed the old layers and become their true "radiant" selves. It may seem like it's too hard or takes too long, but trust me each day that you do something different brings you closer to happiness. You cannot change things or live what you really dream about by going about your day the same old way. Most of us choose fear because that is what we are use to (I call it your comfort zone) and it's easier. Having a negative fear-based mind-set is hard to change at first but it gets easier and easier and you get happier and happier. I am living proof that you can change your life at any age, with the right tools. So when you are in a dark place or having a tough time, remember me and "my story."

I am going to explain how I got here in the next few pages. Sometimes just taking a bath with candles and putting on Laura Mercier almond body cream as I dreamed about my new life did the trick. Ask my friends, I went through days of complete hysteria, fear, and depression that were so bad they would beg me to sleep at their houses. I could not free myself from some of my emotional attachments to an angry ex. Remember it is easier to blame the other person rather than looking at yourself in the mirror, and the more a person fears himself, the meaner they become. The eight months we were separated and living in the same house took an enormous toll on my whole family. Someday I would love to try to have the law changed that allows living under the same roof while going through a divorce *illegal*! I think it is a horrific situation for children to live in. Even though I was trying different yoga classes and trying to eat healthy, I ended up with indigestion, anxiety, sleeping issues, and painful stomach aches, *and* don't forget a benign ovarian tumor. Enough of those memories . . . . moving on.

I began getting in touch with my spirituality. I read a lot about meditation and manifestation. I knew I wasn't the type to sit on the floor chanting *om* for an hour, but there had to be a cool way to do it. I found a coach online who had written a book called *Expect a Miracle* (Kathy Freston). I loved the title. This is how I wanted to live. It's hard to decipher sometimes whether you are living in a fantasy or just manifesting, but this book gave me all of my answers. No, I wasn't crazy for having intuition and feelings about how my life was supposed to be. I just needed to learn how to become myself, so I could get to where I wanted so desperately to be. I read the book, highlighting and turning pages, and loved it. To this day I sleep with a copy next to my bed to remind me to stay on track.

What I learned from Kathy Freston, the now famous vegan, is to just *be still*. Yes, she was speaking my mind exactly! I knew this was true for me as well, it wasn't about running around and trying to find a soul mate or scanning the JDate and Match.com pictures—I never felt comfortable with any of that. Don't take me wrong, I know there are plenty of online success stories, but I always thought I was a little too evolved, real and down to earth and romantic for that. It started becoming a chore to read all of the emails every night plus IMs, and winks were popping up on my BlackBerry all day and it drove me crazy. It began taking my energy away from the very thing I was working so hard on—*being still*. I still believe that love is all about timing and fate. Nothing can keep your true soul mate away from you and you don't have to pressure yourself to be "out" so he finds you. He just will.

In the past I tried to make things happen out of insecurity, desperation, and neediness, which stems from my childhood. (Obviously those relationships didn't turn out so well.) This was the first change I needed to instill in my body, mind, and soul, to get where I wanted to be I had to just *be* and be alone and learn to love myself and reinvent the girl I know I am supposed to be. This wasn't always easy especially when society is constantly telling you the best places to meet men, where to go to meet singles, etc. You can meet a guy anywhere if you are happy, approachable, and confident.

Here's how I learned how to meditate: I ordered Kathy Freston's twenty-minute CDs. They were simple to follow. I would lie on my bed and listen to her tell me how to relax every muscle. I usually tried to do this at the end of my day before my kids came home. I noticed when I picked them up I was much more relaxed and tuned in to seeing how their day was rather than rushing them off to the next activity. I help parents with this in my coaching practice. It's a good lesson especially for younger parents who are consumed with thoughts about their kids getting to the next stage already! It all comes back to being in the moment. My kids have grown so quickly and I have to tell you guys I would do anything to have then spitting up formula on me in the middle of the night! I've learned to appreciate whatever stage they are in and believe me: teenagers and a tween aren't easy. I stay in the moment because ten years from now when I am a grandmother I will be wishing they were teenagers!

The more I manifested the more I began to turn my lonely, scared days into ones of hope and anticipation. I began to realize if all of my dreams are going to come true, I had to really believe in them and I had to make these rituals a routine. I had to get my body, mind, and soul ready for whatever was coming. I knew it wouldn't work if I met the man of my dreams on a day when I wasn't feeling confident. It's a completely different feeling when you feel good about yourself. When you feel secure with who you are, you can be yourself without worrying or caring what anyone thinks. That is how people become drawn to you and see who you really are.

It's important to tell you that I am not a perfect eater—far from it. But 90 percent of the time I do eat healthy or cleanse not only because I want to look good but I want to *feel* good. In my teens and twenties I had binges that lasted weeks and took months to lose. These days a binge lasts half a day because I would rather spend the time working out and eating healthy to get to the next level as opposed to spending a week working off a bad couple of days! To me every day is a miracle day and you never know what can happen. You *must be ready!* You have to love your body to really love yourself. This is key: to have a great relationship with anyone, you must first have a great one with yourself and part of the deal is taking care of your body. When you feel healthy, fit, and sexy, everything about life is better. Making small permanent lifestyle changes (not temporary diets) is what changes your body. We all know how much your relationships suffer when your self-esteem is low. You don't even feel like having sex! When you love yourself and your body, you are less inhibited. I was always a bit of a free spirit, but now especially, I have no problem walking around my bedroom naked!

Little by little, one hour at a time I practiced turning my (fear-based) negative thoughts into positive ones. If I was getting anxious, I would start saying mantras like "Everything works out the way it's supposed to". You have to put your energy into what you want not on what is lacking. Dwelling on the loneliness only makes you feel bad, so why not look forward to meeting the love of your life. Get yourself and your home ready instead of wasting energy feeling lonely. Remember also that negativity and depression look terrible on your face!

Whatever you put your energy into is what you get back. If I worried about the future or complained about the past, it was going to be a crappy day. If I lived in the moment, as I do now, knowing that all I have is today, I can make it a good day. The past is over, even yesterday is over, and tomorrow is unpredictable. We all have no idea what tomorrow will be, nor what five years from now will look like. If you worry about it, it won't turn out so great. If you look forward to it, then good things will happen. Besides, the physical effects of positivity look a lot better on your face and body. Worrying causes wrinkles, frown lines, dryness, etc. As far as weight is concerned, the extra weight most of us are holding onto is from stress and thinking negatively.

The number one thing I stress with my clients is a healthy lifestyle. This isn't only about diet and exercise; it's about your home, your office, and your environment. You can manifest an amazing relationship twenty-four hours a day, but if you feel fat, ugly, and don't love yourself, it will never work! This is all about being ready emotionally, physically, and spiritually (body, mind, soul). You have to be in a good place for life to change. You have to be confident, secure, positive, and ready.

As women, we want to be good at so many things: our jobs, parenthood, marriage and love. In order to be a "superwoman" we have to be physically as well as mentally on top of our game! Think about the difference in your day between a fat day and a thin day. Imagine if you could have 99 percent thin days (let me remind you we are all human and deserve cheat days here and there). Think about how great that would be not only for you but also for everyone in your life. I am not talking about being skinny; I am talking about feeling fit, healthy, energetic, sexy (my favorite word), and happy.

As far as exercise goes, it's not just about "going to the gym," nor is it *ever* about spending hours on a treadmill. We all know people who do this while talking on a cell phone or watching TV—and how is that working for them? Why is this? The only way to really change your body is to put your soul into your workout. The one hour you spend working out should be an intense outer body experience. It should leave you not only sweating but with inspiring thoughts and a clear head. You should be rejuvenated! I have found this in spin classes. You can stand in a gym lifting weights, but I guarantee you as soon as your mind is focused on the muscle you are working *and* you are picturing what you want to look like, your body will begin to change. It's all part of manifesting. The mind is a powerful thing. Tell yourself you are going running just to get it over with or dread going to a class and the results will reflect just that. I have been there. Before I learned to focus, I would increase the running time or change gyms, doing everything to find a quick fix, and if I didn't lose five pounds in a week I was off to the next thing. The truth is you can get results doing almost anything if your mind is in it. You can even spend less time exercising and get better results if you are focused. Working harder for a shorter period of time is more effective than being on a treadmill for two hours watching TV.

Another important part of exercise is doing something you like and challenging yourself. If you don't like something, keep trying different things until you find something you do like. I know for me to love a class there has to be *great* music and an amazing teacher who inspires me more than I do myself. When I was going through my divorce, everyone tried to encourage me to go to yoga classes. I tried classes all over NYC and just didn't like it. I wanted more action and fast music. If I stuck with it I would never have stumbled across Soulcycle. *Body, mind,* and *soul.*

I am sure most of you have probably tried every diet more than once. I'm also sure you have gone back to a diet you were successful with in the past without even realizing if it was so successful you wouldn't be back here? OMG, have I been there and done that. I remember one day being so obsessed with finding my old Diet Center books that I got up in the middle of the night to look for them. There isn't any secret to it. When you make certain lifestyle changes, the weight will come off permanently. These changes are different for everyone and in my coaching business I help people determine what changes need to be made. The changes come if and only if you change your commitment to yourself and to your body. People fail on diets because they let themselves down. You have to be the most important person in the world to yourself. You have to want to look hot and sexy more than anything else. You will change your life completely when you learn how to take care of yourself.

It all goes back to the way you think. Do you actually think if you are eating healthy and you eat a pack (or two) of Dark Reese's that you will go up a size? No, it's when you punish yourself for eating a Reese's that you gain weight. You feel as though you let yourself down and continue on the sugar binge, or add some carbs. Instead, change the way you think about eating a Reese's. How about "I've been eating great, I deserve a treat"? (I call this "flipping it" in my coaching business. You turn the thought into a positive one, creating different energy.) How you eat is all tied in to loving yourself. It's all about self-esteem. Unfortunately most people have it backward and they think they will love themselves when they lose weight. When you love yourself, you want to take care of your body. Your body is a total reflection of how you feel about yourself.

I am now fifty years old and I eat dark chocolate every single day. Yes, I am sure I am premenopausal, but that isn't an excuse to gain ten pounds, it's more of a reason to take care of my body. I'm single and at my prime and am on the verge of being with the love of my life. Why would I blow that? I've worked too hard and getting into my bed every night feels damn good because I'm happy with my body.

In order for you to make some big changes, first make a commitment to your health and body. You can start with something as simple as promising yourself to drink eight glasses of water a day. I hate drinking water but I love how my skin looks when I do and I love that flushed out feeling from peeing all day! Once you get used to it, it becomes routine. As with anything else, doing it is so much easier than dreading it! I now take a multivitamin and omega-3 every day and recently my gynecologist recommended I start taking calcium and vitamin D. Start looking into what supplements you might need and try them.

Another simple change I made, with huge results, has been kicking the Diet Coke habit and switching to green tea. In the winter I drink it hot; in the summer, iced. People who know me rarely see me without it! It's great for your metabolism and it has antioxidants. Another habit of mine is eating handfuls of almonds throughout the day. I used to eat handfuls of M&Ms, but now I prefer almonds and blueberries. Another trick of mine is roasted veggies for a nighttime snack. I make trays and trays of them and keep them in the refrigerator and warm them up when I'm hanging out at night. You might be thinking, *Just what I want while I'm watching TV is a roasted carrot!* but you know what? It tastes really good roasted with olive oil and sea salt, and waking up and feeling good putting on my jeans is worth it!

I've recently started helping my clients with things like cleaning out their kitchens, closets, offices, and homes. I strongly believe that a less cluttered living space means a less cluttered life. My home is now clutter free, which makes me stress free. I chose to decorate it very sleek and modern with shag rugs and a lot of candles. I always have fresh flowers and candles lit. I love the energy here. It is *me*. When you clear out your living space, you can come home at the end of the day and just relax. It's like going to a nice hotel. The same goes for your space at work. How can you possibly work effectively with junk and old coffee cups on your desk? Clean it up and make way for productive work!

When I meet my NYC clients for appointments, I usually meet them in a great hotel in a lobby or lounge. I have my favorite spots. This is a relaxing way for me to work and sets the tone so my clients feel comfortable with me. I am not a corporate type of person and the thought of sitting at a desk doesn't really appeal to me. I also prefer not to have my clients lying on a couch as I take notes sitting in a chair. I like to focus and connect with what they are telling me and how they feel. It's important to me that my clients know about me and my life. After all, if I got here, I can get them here too.

My greatest challenge (the one with the greatest rewards), has been learning to change my negative thoughts to positive ones. Like I mentioned before, we all have our dark times and have suffered one way or another. I wanted to move on from my past but needed to deal with the pain of it so it wouldn't be in my body anymore. This is where coaching comes in. It's all about moving forward. You set goals and envision what you want your life to look like and then learn to use certain tools to get there. Having overcome so much has given me the insight to help my clients. Hearing my stories gives them hope. If you saw me two years ago, you probably would not even know it was me. I was lost, scared, confused. When going through my divorce, there were days I almost gave up. As I got stronger, I got smarter and realized it was only my thoughts that were terrifying me and that nothing bad was going to happen . . . I was moving toward the life I wanted.

I no longer wake up sad in the mornings but things are different now. Yes, I still have bad days, but I know they are just that: bad days. I know the next day will be better because I have the mind-set to make it that way. We have the power to make things as bad or as good as we want them to be. Yes, in two short years I went through a divorce, which would have been enough on its own, put my dog to sleep, had a benign tumor, sent my son to college, went through my parents' divorce, and sold my house, but look where I am now. Sometimes I just think to myself, *Holy shit, I made it. I left a relationship that was not good for me. I took the high road and never gave in, never looked back.* Yes, it was tough going through the recovery stage, but I did it. Now I just walk away from toxic people. It feels better to have compassion for the wounded rather than take it personally. I no longer spend time and energy on the past.

When you begin to love yourself it shows. It shows in the way you walk, talk, eat, shop, communicate, and even have sex. Everything and anything is affected by this state of mind. I know when I am feeling radiant and magnetic by the way people look at me. I am at the point where I can turn on my heartlight and get so into it that I can feel people looking at me with admiration. When you are happy, people know it and they want to know why and how. The only way I can describe it is *I am plugged in to who I am.* Instead of racing or "getting" through my day like I used to, I take the time to look at the faces of whomever I am talking to, I have more patience and listen to my kids. I like hearing from my friends about what is going on in their lives without being jealous that they are still married.

When you feel good on the inside, it shows. However I do have some beauty tips that I like to share that work for me. I already mentioned facial acupuncture. Aimee Raupp has given me a whole new confidence as far as my skin is concerned. I have sessions with Aimee twice a month religiously. I am someone who has always been afraid of needles but this is different. It doesn't hurt at all. The first half hour I lie on a table with the needles and a heat lamp on my stomach and go into the most amazing trance. I am just completely knocked out for twenty minutes. When I wake up, I feel totally rejuvenated and recharged. Afterward, Aimee either puts collagen on my face or an egg-white mask and when we are finished I swear I could go to a party without any makeup on! It's an incredible part of my journey.

Taking a bath is a great way to end the day. It's so important to have some "me" time and a bath is an easy, inexpensive way to do it. I have great bubble baths and creams I love to use and I light candles. Each one is lit for a different part of my life and when I light them I say little prayers. There is one for my kids, one for my career, one for my family and friends, and one for my future soul mate who will eventually be in the tub with me. (Think *Pretty Women*.)

When I began my journey about three years ago, I went to Laura Bruen for a photo shoot. I was nervous and not very confident but she saw something in me through her lens that was revealed in some amazing pictures. I realized what other people saw was not what I always saw. She captured my spirit that was hidden behind years of self-doubt. I began to peel away the layers on my own and every six months I have Laura take my picture to mark my progress and remind me who I really am.

As you already know, there is always some kind of dark chocolate at my disposal! I either have Godiva, Whole Foods dark chocolate, or the more popular kind I love like dark Reese's or dark M&Ms. I have learned to love the little things in life and this is what makes me happy. It doesn't all have to be so complicated. If a relationship isn't working or you hate your job, then fix things or move on. Life is short and the longer you live in fear, the longer it will take to have the life you really want. Take chances, say what you really want to say, do things a little differently. There really isn't anything to be afraid of. Things either work out or they don't. When they don't work out, learn the lesson and move on to bigger and better. I have no idea where my life is going, but I know one thing. I'm finally headed in the right direction and I am happy.

Made in the USA
Lexington, KY
03 September 2012